# APPLIQUE APPLIED

## OVER 20 STUNNING PROJECTS IN MACHINE APPLIQUE, EMBROIDERY AND QUILTING

# EILEEN CAMPBELL

## A Lothian Book

# Dedication

To my Aunt Mary, for her constant love and inspiration.

## Acknowledgments

My very special and sincere thanks to my wonderful family – my sons and daughters-in-law, Neil and Sarah, Alan and Katie-Anne, Derek and Alison, and grandson, Lachlan – for their practical support and encouragement at all times, but especially during the writing of this book.

In particular, I thank Derek for the quilt diagrams and Katie-Anne, Sarah and Lachlan for being my models. To Neil my heartfelt thanks for his patience and computer expertise when writing the text.

Thankyou to Lachlan Campbell, my niece Amanda Beet and her husband Andrew, and my aunt, Mary Chessell, for the loan of their quilts. Also to Michael Phillips for his excellent photographs and to Glenda Frost and Ernie Pietsch for all their encouragement and enthusiasm.

A Lothian Book
Thomas C. Lothian Pty Ltd
11 Munro Street, Port Melbourne, Victoria 3207

National Library of Australia
Cataloguing-in-publication data:

Campbell, Eileen, 1939–
Appliqué applied

ISBN 0 85091 629 1

1. Appliqué 2. Machine appliqué I. Title.
(Series: Lothian Australian craft series).

746.445

Cover and text design by Zoë Murphy
Photographs by Michael Phillips
Typeset in Australia by Image Makers
Printed by Singapore National Printers Ltd

# Contents

# Introduction

According to one dictionary, appliqué is the ornamentation formed by sewing or otherwise applying one material to another.

Appliqué has been used in many forms for centuries; from decorations as diverse as beads, fish scales, leaves and bark to the more conventional method of fabric applied to fabric.

Appliqué using a machine satin stitch has only been possible since the invention of the zigzag sewing machine. This book deals mostly with the technique for appliqué that involves the use of the bonding medium Vliesofix® for the appliqué pieces and a stabiliser, such as Tearaway®, on the back of the work.

The projects range from simple, single-shape motifs through to the more challenging, multi-piece birds on one of the jackets and Magpie quilt. The use of simple machine or hand embroidery and the addition of trimmings such as beads and ribbons are what give life to these appliqués. Some of the projects are machine quilted. It is possible to do this quite easily if you follow the instructions, or you can quilt by hand, if you prefer. There are also suggestions for glued appliqués and stencilling.

Any of the motifs in this book can be adapted for your own projects or may inspire you to create your own designs. When you follow the instructions for a project you will find that your own imagination will introduce a unique, personal touch to your creations.

I recommend that you familiarise yourself thoroughly with the general instructions that follow before embarking on any project. In this way you can create your appliqué with minimum fuss and maximum pleasure.

Relax and enjoy the limitless possibilities of *Appliqué Applied*.

# MATERIALS & TECHNIQUES

I have already said this in my introduction, but do read this section carefully before beginning a project.

## Fabrics

All the projects in this book are made with 100 per cent cotton fabrics, which are very easy to work with. Polycotton, silk and synthetic fabrics can also be used, of course, but you may find some of them a little more difficult to handle if you have not done appliqué before. Before you begin, wash, then dry all your fabrics in a drier to test for colour-fastness and also to be sure that fabrics will not shrink at different rates when the finished articles are washed later.

Once you have done a little appliqué, you will probably find yourself looking at fabrics in a different light. One pattern might suggest leaves or tree trunks, while another suggests bird's feathers, animal fur or even snail shells. If you see a fabric you think will be useful, then even 20–25 cm (8–10 in) will make quite a few appliqués. It is easy to become addicted to collecting fabrics. Sort them into colours and types, storing them in labelled or clear plastic boxes, so that you can find them easily for your projects.

## Designs

As well as using the designs in this book, you can make up your own. Children's colouring books can be a good source of designs, as are any simplified shapes from every day objects.

Take designs from your own photographs of flowers, animals or scenery, or from a suitable picture, by first tracing over the main outline of the object. Then include other major lines or highlights, reducing the picture to its simplest form. Remember that each line you draw will have to be stitched.

Draw your appliqué designs to the correct size for the project so you can trace directly over them. If the original motif is not the correct size for what you need, then it is easily altered. For example, if the original motif fits into a 10-cm (4-in) square and you need a 20-cm (8-in) square, enlarge it in the following way.

1 Trace the motif on another piece of paper so that you do not damage the original.
2 Draw a sixteen-square grid over the design. Each square will be 2.5 cm (1 in) x 2.5 cm (1 in) and there will be four squares on each side.
3 Draw another sixteen square grid, but make each square 5 cm (2 in) x 5 cm (2 in). This will give a square that is 20 cm (8 in) x 20 cm (8 in).
4 Copy the shapes from the small grid on the large one. Even if you think you cannot draw, you will find this very easy as it is done a little at a time.

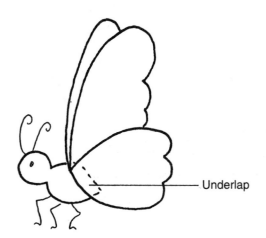

Underlap

Cut body from second fabric
Embroider details after satin stitching

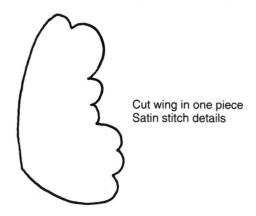

Cut wing in one piece
Satin stitch details

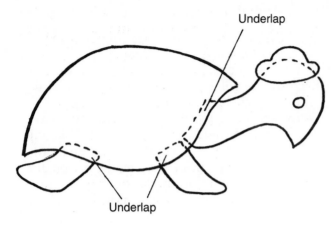

Underlap

Underlap

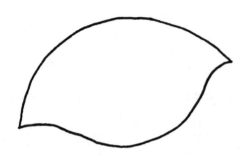

Cut shell from first fabric

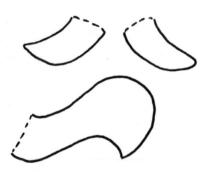

Cut head and feet from second fabric

Cut hat from third fabric

If you have access to a photocopier that will enlarge or reduce, then the job is made even more simple.

Having designed your appliqué you must then decide how to fit the pieces together (unless it is just one simple shape).

When two shapes touch, one of them must have a seam allowance or underlap so that all pieces can be firmly stitched to the backing fabric without gaps or raw edges showing. In most cases, the underlap is added to the shape closest to the background. All you need to do is draw in a dotted line for the underlap extension on your original design then include it on your tracing. The design then needs to be separated and its component pieces traced individually.

All the designs in this book have the underlap allowance shown by a dotted line.

## Vliesofix®

Vliesofix® is a double-sided, fusible webbing with tracing paper on one side. It makes appliqué very simple, provided you remember one thing. **Your design must be drawn in reverse on the Vliesofix®.**

To reverse the image to draw on the Vliesofix®, hold or tape your design to a window so that the light shines through it and you will be able to trace your design lines on the reverse of the paper very easily. If you have access to a light box, this step is accomplished even more easily, and with less strain on your arms.

Step-by-step instructions for using Vliesofix® are as follows.

1 Reverse the motif as explained above and trace it on the smooth, paper side of the Vliesofix®.
2 Cut out the motif in Vliesofix®, leaving a small margin all around. If you have many flowers or leaves to be cut from the same fabric, you can trace them in a block and handle them all as one at this stage.
3 Using a medium heat, iron your motif or motifs to the back of the appliqué fabric with the rough side of the Vliesofix® against the fabric.
4 Cut out the shapes exactly.
5 Decide where the cut out appliqué shapes are to be placed on the background fabric, making sure that all the underlaps are in place.
6 Peel off the backing paper from the Vliesofix® and iron your design in place. Press with the iron, rather than slide it across the pieces, so that the pieces are not disturbed.

7 Back your work with a stabiliser such as Tearaway® or iron-on Vilene. What you use will depend on the project you are working on. You are then ready to stitch.

8 Stitch the appliqué pieces in place. The stabiliser can be torn off afterwards (see below).

> **Note:** When you have designs with many flowers or leaves, it is easiest to cut out a few more than you think you will need. You can then adjust the design on the background fabric, adding or subtracting pieces until you are satisfied. Keep any spare pieces as they are very handy for small projects like cards, or they can be used in another design.

# Stabiliser

All the projects in this book were made using an iron-on stabiliser of some description on the back of the appliquéd sections. Using a stabiliser gives you a very firm surface to work on, making it much easier to keep your work flat and the stitching even.

There is a range of iron-on stabilisers on the market, so the problem is which to choose for a particular project.

If you are making clothing or quilts, then you do not want to end up with a very stiff appliqué area. In this case, choose a stabiliser that can be torn away easily after the stitching is completed. Tearaway® is one such product.

If, on the other hand, your appliqué is on something like a belt, the flap on the pocket of a bag or free-standing, like the butterflies on page 28, then a permanent stabiliser such as iron-on Vilene can be used.

# The sewing machine

Always make sure your machine is totally free of lint around the bobbin case. Clean it thoroughly before using it.

The needle should be sharp and the correct size for the thread and fabric. A size 80 needle is good for most work.

Use an appliqué or clear plastic foot, so that you can see your work easily.

If your machine has a dial to adjust the pressure on the presser foot, then release the pressure for satin-stitching the appliqué as it allows you more freedom of movement with your fabric.

# Tension

The top tension will probably need adjusting. You are trying to achieve a smooth satin stitch without any bobbin thread showing on either side. To do this, loosen the top tension a little. For example, if the normal setting is 4, then reduce it to 3. If your machine just has + or – on the tension dial then move it towards the – (minus) sign.

Stitch a test piece with the top and bobbin threads in different colours, then take it out of the machine and look at the back. You should have the top thread colour showing down both sides as a narrow band and the bobbin thread in between. If the top thread is not being pulled through enough, loosen the top tension a little more and try again.

On some machines, threading the bobbin thread through the special hole for making buttonholes has the same effect as loosening the tension, on others there is a buttonhole-stitch setting. Check your machine manual.

# Threads

You will achieve the best results if you use a machine embroidery rayon thread such as Madeira, Isofil, Sulky or DMC. These threads give a lovely sheen to your work. You can also use ordinary polycotton threads, but you may not get as even a satin stitch. You will also find the stitch length adjustment will not be as fine as with the rayon threads. Avoid using cheap bargain polyester threads. They are short-staple threads, which will not produce the fine satin stitch needed for appliqué.

There is also a wide range of metallic threads available. Madeira metallic threads give excellent results. When you use metallic threads it is best to use a Metalfil needle. This has a larger eye, which will help stop the metallic threads snapping.

If your tension has been adjusted correctly (see above), you should be able to use either black or white thread in the bobbin and not have it show on the top. This will save changing bobbins every time you change the top thread. Bobbinfil, a Madeira thread made specially for use in the bobbin, works well as it is compatible with the rayon threads. If you still have the bobbin thread showing through on the top, then one solution is to put the same thread on top and in the bobbin. The bobbin thread will still show, but you will not notice it. If you have to use rayon thread in the bobbin, wind the bobbin slowly so you do not stretch or break the thread.

# Satin stitching

Your sewing machine manual should tell you how to adjust your machine for satin stitch, so always consult that first.

What you are trying to achieve is a zigzag stitch that is close enough together to appear to be a solid line, but not so close that the stitches bunch up and jam the machine. Use two layers of fabric with stabiliser on the back as a test piece, as this most closely resembles what you will be working on.

For most appliqué the width of the stitch will be about 2–2.5 mm. It is difficult to appliqué with a width less than 1 mm as the stitch becomes too narrow to hold the appliqué in place. Your stitches should rest mostly on the piece being appliquéd, only just coming over onto the background fabric.

The length should be set very fine, but still with enough length so that if you let go of the fabric the feed dogs (the little teeth under the presser foot) will push the fabric through the machine without any problem.

Plan the stitching order beginning with shapes that are furthest back and work your way to the front. Most starting and stopping points will be covered by subsequent stitching. For example, on the tortoise, the legs and head will be stitched first. When the tortoise shell is stitched the beginning and end of the stitching on the head and legs will be covered, leaving only the starting and stopping points on the shell to deal with.

Satin stitch along the edge of each appliqué. Leave a 5-cm (2-in) tail of thread at the beginning and end of each line of stitches. If the ends will be covered by additional rows of stitching, you can clip off the ends. If not, pull the loose threads to the back and secure them. Sometimes it is possible to do two or three fastening stitches at the beginning and end of the stitching instead of pulling threads through.

## Curves

Your aim is to always sew at right angles to the edge of the appliqué piece you are stitching.

1 Start by sewing the first few stitches, continue until you reach the point where you need to change the angle to go around a curve.
2 Stop the machine with the needle in the fabric on the outside edge of the curve.
3 Lift the presser foot and turn the fabric slightly. This is called 'pivoting'.
4 Lower the presser foot and sew a few more stitches.

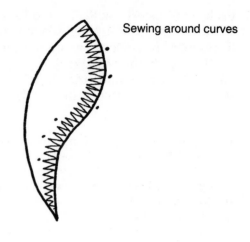

Sewing around curves

• Pivot points for curves

5 Continue in this manner, sewing, stopping, pivoting, sewing, until the curve is completed.

With experience you will find you can control your stitching at a fair speed, you can then eliminate some of the stopping and starting by turning your work as you go.

## Points

This technique will give a tapered point.

1 Near the apex of the point, decrease the stitch width. If it is a very sharp point, you will be enclosing both raw edges at the same time.

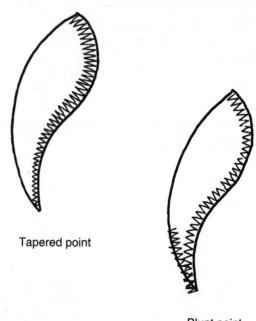

Tapered point

Blunt point

**2** At the very tip of the point, raise the presser foot and turn your work by pivoting, leaving the needle in the fabric.

**3** After you have pivoted, lower the presser foot and raise the needle out of the fabric.

**4** Raise the presser foot again but only enough to move the fabric so that the needle is close to the point again.

**5** Continue sewing, gradually increasing the stitch width to its original size.

This technique will give a blunt point.

If you cannot increase and decrease the stitch width on your machine gradually, use the above technique without decreasing. The stitches will overlap at the point, and you will get a blunt point, but this is also effective. It is also much easier to stitch.

## Trouble-shooting

**1** Even though you have loosened the top tension, you will sometimes find that the satin stitching pulls inwards giving a slightly bunched up or tunnel effect in the fabric. This is not an ideal situation, as it will distort the background fabric and the appliqué.

To counteract this, as you stitch hold the first two fingers of your left hand in a V shape on either side of the presser foot, exerting pressure away from both sides of the presser foot. This will stop your work forming a tunnel. Your left hand is the one you use most to control your work and, even though this may seem strange at first, it is worth practising until you can do it comfortably. Your right hand is then free to change the stitch width as you sew.

**2** Sometimes it does not matter if your stitching goes a little off line and moves too far onto the appliqué, for example, if it is a leaf or a flower and the basic shape is not altered appreciably. If this is the case, lift the excess appliqué fabric with your fingernail, then use a very sharp pair of small scissors to trim the piece off.

If trimming the appliqué will spoil the shape, or if you have stitched too far off the appliqué so that it is no longer held down, then you must take the stitching out and re-stitch it. The simplest method is to turn your work to the back and with a small pair of sharp scissors, cut through the satin-stitching in the bobbin thread. Turn the work to the right side, and pull the top thread above where you have cut. It will unravel like magic.

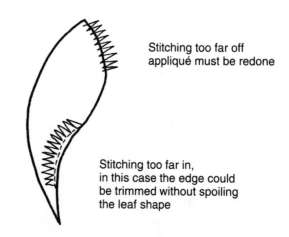

Stitching too far off appliqué must be redone

Stitching too far in, in this case the edge could be trimmed without spoiling the leaf shape

Problems

## Test swatches

As each piece of work can be different, using different fabrics, etc., it is best to make a test swatch for each project using exactly the fabrics and threads planned for the finished article. Do not miss out on this step, it will save mistakes on the real thing and, maybe, hours of unpicking.

# Embroidery

Many of the projects are embroidered. This can be done by hand, by machine or a combination of both. Very simple stitches have been used in both techniques, so it is not difficult to embellish your work with maximum effect.

## By hand

You will only need three basic stitches to decorate the projects in this book.

**1** Stem stitch is used to decorate flowers, stems or add highlights to creatures of all sorts.

**2** Chain stitch is used for bird's legs. This stitch can be used in combination with machine satin stitch.

**3** French knots are used for flower stamens and on butterfly wings.

Stem stitch

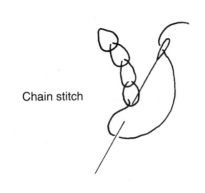

Chain stitch

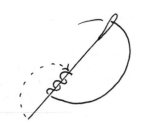

French knot

### Needles

A size 75 or 80 needle is good to work with. At first you could practise using a size 90, as this breaks less readily. If you are using metallic thread, then a Metalfil needle should be used. Machine embroidery needles are also available now in sizes 75 and 90; these have a groove down the front side of the needle.

A handy hint for keeping track of machine needles is to have a special, labelled pincushion. With machine embroidery there are times when you should change from one needle to another, for example, from normal size 80 needle to a Metalfil one. Once the needles are out of their original packets, it is difficult to tell them apart. Mark the pincushion with the various sizes and types of needles and as you change them store the needles not in use in their appropriate place on the pincushion.

Pin cushion marked to help you to keep track of your machine needles

Q = quilting needles

E = embroidery needles

M = Metalfil needles

### By machine

If you have not done machine embroidery before, do not be daunted as this can open up a whole new world for you. It is rather like using a needle instead of a pencil as your drawing tool and, in many ways, it is much easier as you do not have to draw precisely. For example, your lines can wander all over a flower and still look most effective.

To begin, you will need to be able to lower the feed dogs on your machine or be able to cover them with a plate. Many machines have a button on the side, somewhere near the bobbin case, to enable you to lower the feed dogs. Check your machine manual if you are not sure or ask someone who sells your brand of sewing machine. Having lowered or covered the feed dogs, set your machine for straight stitching and your stitch length and width to 0. The tension setting should be normal.

### Darning foot

Although it is possible to take the normal sewing foot off the machine and embroider without a foot at all, it is much safer and easier to use a darning foot. If you are working without a hoop, it is necessary to have a darning foot to hold the fabric while the stitches are being made.

A darning foot usually has a spring that allows it to move up and down as you sew; it gives support to the needle as it makes the stitch, but allows you to move the fabric freely at the same time.

On some Husqvarna machines there is a special darning setting, so you can turn to the relevant symbol for free machining or darning, which regulates the pressure of the machine foot on the fabric. Some Pfaff machines have a cradle position on the presser lever that lets you free-machine stitch without lowering the foot right onto the fabric. Check with your machine manual or sewing machine dealer, as different makes and models have different adjustments.

Whichever machine and darning foot you have, it is essential to lower the presser foot lever before you begin sewing, otherwise you will just end up with a terrible tangle of threads on the underside of your work.

### Using a hoop

For much of the embroidery on these projects, you may not need to use a hoop providing you are embroidering a small area and you have a stabiliser on the back of your work. This should be a firm enough surface to work on.

If you are embroidering a larger area such as a group of flowers or the gum blossoms on the cushions or quilt, then putting your work in a hoop will give you a better surface to work on and the finished embroidery will lie flat.

Working with a hoop for machine embroidery is done in the opposite way to hand embroidery. The fabric is placed at the bottom of the hoop, so that it will lie flat on the bed of the machine.

A plastic and metal spring hoop – either 13 cm (5 in) or 18 cm (7 in) – is very easy to work with. It can be moved quickly and easily from one area to another and with your fabric already stabilised, you do not have to be so concerned about the tension in the hoop. If you are doing more elaborate embroidery, especially without a stabiliser, then you will need to use a wooden hoop with a binding on the inside ring, which can be tightened with a screw at the side. However this is beyond the scope of this book.

To use a spring hoop, lay the plastic ring on a flat surface, place your fabric over the top and, squeezing the two handles on the metal spring together, fit the spring into the plastic ring so that the fabric is stretched evenly all around. There will be one place just in front of the spring handles where you are unable to get correct tension in the fabric. Just be aware of this and position the area to be embroidered away from it.

If you are new to machine embroidery, it is worth practising on some sample swatches until you get the feel for it.

### Instructions

Begin machine embroidering as follows:

1 Lower or cover the feed dogs.
2 Set your machine for straight stitching, stitch length and width to 0, tension setting normal.
3 Lower the presser bar.
4 Bring the bobbin thread to the top by taking one stitch and pulling on the top thread to bring the bobbin thread up.
5 Hold both threads to the back of your work and make two or three stitches, which will hold both threads. You can now cut the threads off.
6 Begin to stitch, moving your work in any direction. By co-ordinating the movement of your work with your hands and the speed of your sewing with the foot pedal, you will be able to control the size, length and direction of your stitching. It is best if you can maintain a fairly fast machining speed, but this will come, with practice.

It is not necessary to turn your work, as you can stitch in any direction. For example, if you are embroidering gum blossom in a hoop and the hoop handles are on the right side, move your hoop backwards, forwards, sideways and diagonally, but always keep the handles on the right.

### Machine embroidery used in the projects

Most of the designs are continuous stitching, but the special effects are worked as follows:

1 Flowers: begin in the flower centre and work around and between each petal in your chosen design.
2 Leaves: begin at the base of the leaf, stitch the centre vein and on the return stitching, the diagonals for the smaller veins.
3 Gum Blossoms: using gold thread, begin with a circle, then radiate lines all the way around, coming back to where you started. Change to red thread and machine over the blossoms again, leaving enough space for the gold thread

Flowers: begin in the centre and work around in a continuous line

Leaves: begin at the base of the leaf and stitch the main vein. Work the diagonal veins on your return

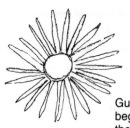

Gum blossoms: with gold thread, begin by stitching the centre circle and then stitch the radiating lines. Change to red thread and stitch over the gold thread, allowing it to show through

Complete the flower centre

to shine through. Machine the centre of each blossom.

4 Butterfly wing veins: these can be done as a continuous line before attaching or stitching the body part. The feelers are done separately.

## Beading

Seed and larger beads, with baubles and sequins can add a sparkle to your work. They are best used on wall hangings or on special clothing that will be laundered carefully.

You will need a needle that is fine enough to go through the beads. A size 10 Between or quilting needle is usually good. You will also need fine strong thread. Madeira monofilament, although difficult to knot, is strong and goes through fine seed beads easily. Because it is clear, it does not show. You could also use a fine thread in a colour that matches the beads.

With the gum blossoms, place beads at intervals around the edge of each flower, fastening off after each blossom although you need not necessarily cut the thread. Fastening off after every blossom safeguards against too many beads becoming loose if they are accidentally snagged with use.

A single sequin and a bead makes a very easy and effective bird's eye. Beads can also be used to highlight shapes such as snail or tortoise-shell markings. The tortoises in the wall hangings have bead necklaces that hang free, and are just attached at each end.

When pressing work with beading on it, avoid the beads or place the work with the right side down on a towel and press carefully. Sequins are best not pressed at all as they will flatten or buckle under the heat.

## Quilting by machine

This book cannot possibly cover all the intricacies of hand and machine quilting, however the majority of projects have been quilted in straight lines by machine. Even the quilts, although the ones photographed are a little more complicated, could also be adapted to quilting in straight lines.

For successful quilting you need to prepare well. There are three layers to a quilt: the top, the batting or wadding and the backing, all must be held firmly and evenly together.

To put a quilt or wall hanging together ready for quilting, follow the steps below.

1 Prepare a backing (you will have to join the fabric for a large quilt) that is at least 5 cm (2 in) bigger all around than the quilt top.
2 Lay the backing out, wrong side up, on a smooth flat surface such as a large table or the floor.
3 Pull the edges of the backing taut but do not stretch them and tape the backing at the corners and in the centre of each side.
4 The batting is placed on top and also taped in place. It should cover the backing. If you are using pre-cut packaged backing, roll it out, smooth it carefully over the backing, then tape.

If you are using batting bought by the metre (yard) that has to be joined, butt the edges to be joined and sew them together with a diagonal basting stitch. Do not overlap the batting sections or you will have a ridge in the finished quilt.

5 Press the quilt top thoroughly. You will not be able to press it again once it is in place.
6 Place quilt top, right side up, on top of the batting, making sure the centre of the quilt top edges line up with the centre points on the edges of the backing. Tape it in place.
7 Beginning in the centre and working out towards the edges, place 2.5 cm (1 in) safety pins 8–10 cm (3–4 in) apart over the entire quilt. Try not to place the pins where you intend to stitch (except for the Cornelli stitching where this is unavoidable). For a large quilt you will need 400 to 500 pins.
8 Remove the tape and you are ready to quilt.

## Threads

For a quilting line that gives texture without making a feature of the thread, use Madeira Monofil. This is a nylon monofilament thread that is either clear or smoke coloured. Monofilament thread is quite springy and difficult to tie. The easiest way to stop and start your stitching is to bring your stitch length to 0 for the first or last five or six stitches. Alternatively you can use a polycotton thread that tones with the background. In the bobbin use a polycotton thread that tones with the backing.

## Needles

A size 80 needle or a machine quilting needle size 75 to 90 (available from sewing machine supply shops) is best.

## Sewing-machine feet

For straight line quilting, either in the ditch, as decoration or gentle curves, a walking foot is excellent and should be used if possible. A walking foot feeds the three layers of fabric evenly through the machine. Some Pfaff machines have an even-feed foot built into the machine instead of a walking foot and if your machine has this, it should be engaged. For outline quilting or the Cornelli quilting on the large quilts, a darning foot is necessary.

## Marking

Your choice of marker depends on the colour of the fabric and what type of design you have to mark. Test your marker on a scrap of fabric first to check for visibility and how easily the marks can be removed. Some methods are listed below.

1 Silver or fine, H-lead pencil.
2 Coloured pencil a couple of shades darker than your fabric.
3 Water-soluble blue pen. There are a few brands on the market; make sure the one you choose is soluble and do not use near a heat source as that may fix the markings permanently.
4 Tailor's chalk or pencil.
5 Quilter's tape 6 mm ($\frac{1}{4}$ in) (wide available from quilting supply shops).
6 Chalk wheel.

Use the following technique to mark a simple quilting design on a project such as a wall hanging.

1 Find the centre of each side and connect to the centre point on the adjoining side to form a diamond shape.
2 Decide how far apart you want your quilting lines to be, somewhere between 5 cm (2 in) and 9.5 cm (3$\frac{1}{2}$ in) works well. Measure in from your first quilting line and construct the next diamond shape. Repeat as often as necessary.

Mark diamond shapes on your quilt for machine quilting: do not stitch over appliqués or embroidery

**Note:** When quilting do not quilt over any appliquéd shapes or embroidery. Quilt up to a shape, finish off, lift the presser foot and begin again on the other side. When you have finished the quilting, cut the threads between these points on the front and back.

**3** If you have borders, lozenge-shaped curves can be marked quite easily. Begin by measuring the length to be quilted. Divide it into sections approximately 9.5 cm (3½ in) to 18 cm (7 in) and make a template from a thin card or plastic that you can trace around. The lozenge shapes can be machined in two long curving lines (see diagram).

Quilting in the ditch needs no marking as you follow the seam line. Stitch on the low side of the seam and the actual quilting stitches will be almost invisible.

## Stitching

**1** If you can control the pressure exerted by the presser foot on your machine, then release the pressure for quilting.

**2** Increase the stitch length to 3 or 3.5 mm for quilting with a walking foot.

**3** For small pieces, the work can be handled flat under the machine, for larger pieces or bed-sized quilts, roll the two opposite sides of the quilt towards the centre leaving the area to be stitched exposed.

**4** For all quilting, begin in the centre and work towards the edges, stitching across half of the quilt each time. Place the quilt under the machine and, beginning at the centre, unroll the quilt as you stitch along each line towards the edge. Turn the quilt and repeat for the other side. It is best to do all areas in one direction: for example, do all lengthways stitching first, then turn the quilt and stitch at right angles across your first stitching.

**5** Remove all the safety pins.

**6** Bind the quilt or wall hanging (see Finishing your quilt on page 15).

## Free-machine quilting

By setting the machine as for machine embroidery (that is, dropping the feed dogs, etc.) you can outline your appliqués by stitching them approximately 3 mm (⅛ in) from the edge of the motif.

You can also do a Cornelli-type design by using the machine stitching to scribble or doodle over

Begin here when stitching both lines

A

B

the fabric. You may have to tighten the top tension on your machine (sometimes quite a deal) to achieve good results. To tighten, turn the tension dial to a higher number or towards the + sign if your machine does not have numbers. Work a test piece first using the same fabrics and batting as for your project.

14

When you are free-machining a Cornelli-type design around appliqués, plan your stitching so that you have as few stops and starts as possible (although you will have to stop to take out the safety pins). Always try to leave yourself a pathway to get out as you machine around your designs.

## Tying a quilt

Instead of quilting, an alternative method is to tie the quilt layers together with either very narrow ribbons or lengths of thread. This technique can also be used in conjunction with machine or hand quilting. The ties can be on the front or on the back, depending on the look you want to achieve. You will probably need a tapestry needle and a pair of pliers to pull ribbons through the fabric.

## Finishing a quilt

If you have enough backing fabric, you can finish the quilt by turning it to the front and slip stitching it in place. First, trim the batting evenly all around leaving just enough to fill the binding.

You can also finish the edges by trimming the backing to approximately 1.5 cm (½ in) or 2.5 cm (1 in), then cutting strips of fabric long enough to bind each side. The strips will need to be twice the width of your trimmed batting and backing plus 1.5 cm (½ in) for the seams. Attach the strips by sewing to the top side of the quilt with the right sides together, mitring the corners neatly. Turn the binding over the edge, fold the seam allowance under and slip stitch it in place on the back.

## Hanging a quilt

To hang a quilt or wall hanging, you will need either loops or a rod pocket on the back. Attach these by hand last of all.
You make a rod pocket as follows:

1 Cut a piece of fabric 20 cm (8 in) by the width of your quilt or wall hanging.
2 Make a 1-cm (½-in) hem along the shorter ends.
3 Fold the fabric in half lengthways with the wrong sides together, and stitch with a 6-mm (¼-in) seam allowance.
4 Press it, putting the seam in the centre of one side.
5 Attach the pocket to the quilt by hand, slip stitching both long sides but leaving a slight bulge on the top to accommodate the rod. It should be 1 cm (½ in) from the top of the quilt.

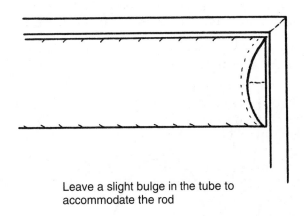

Leave a slight bulge in the tube to accommodate the rod

## No-sewing appliqué

It is possible to appliqué without sewing; instead of satin stitching the edges, use one of the dimensional fabric and craft paint pens, such as Polymark®.

1 Follow the instructions for applying appliqué shapes using Vliesofix® on page 6, but do not use any stabiliser on the back.
2 Embroider any details before using the paint. (If you machine embroider you will need stabiliser on the back.)
3 Apply the paint around the edges, carefully sealing all the raw edges. Allow to dry flat for six to eight hours.
4 Wait at least 72 hours before laundering.

## Stencilling

Some of the designs in this book, including the flowers, frogs, tortoises or snails, are suitable for stencilling.

To make a stencil, use either a medium-weight card, about the thickness of a manilla folder or the Mylar® plastic available from specialist or craft outlets that is made especially for this purpose.

You will need a stencil knife to cut out the designs. Make sure you do not cut directly on a table or bench. Place thick card or a wad of newspapers underneath as a cutting surface.

You will also need a stencil brush, which has short, stubby bristles and paint suited to the medium you are working on, either fabric or paper.

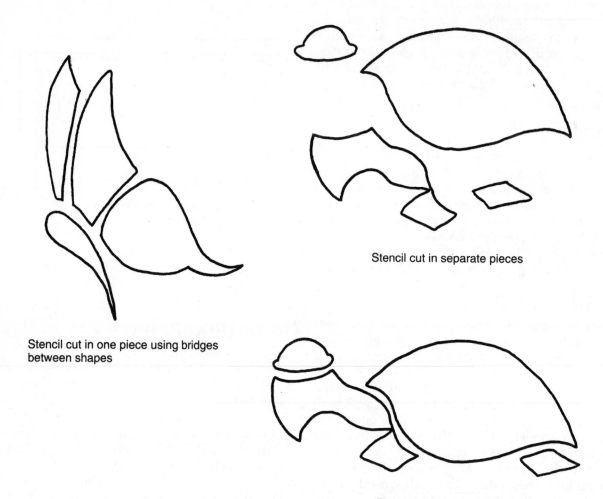

Stencil cut in separate pieces

Stencil cut in one piece using bridges between shapes

Pieces joined when stencilling

The butterfly is stencilled in one colour with bridges between the various shapes. If designs such as tortoises or snails are to be stencilled in two colours, cut the parts of the design separately and align the design as you paint the areas in different colours.

If you want to embellish or embroider (if you machine embroider you will need a stabiliser on the back) the motifs painted on fabric, allow the paint to dry and set your stencilled design first. The method you use for setting the design will depend on the paint you use. Follow the manufacturer's instructions.

TOP: *The three-dimensional butterflies make the* Blue Meadow Place Mats *and* Serviette Rings *a most unusual and eye-catching place setting. Choose colours to tone with your china. They would also make a wonderful gift with a matching card.*

BOTTOM: *The* Decorative Bookmarks, Butterfly Picture, Floral Glasses Case *and the* Box with Jewelled Fan Lid *are all fairly simple to make.*

*Australian themes to add an original touch to your decor. The* Brolga Wall
Hanging *and* Cushion *and the* Gum Blossom Cushion *can be mixed
and matched to great effect.*

# PROJECTS

The design motifs are all actual size, with the exception of those on pages 39, 42, 46 and 51–4; which are 80 per cent of actual size. The brolga that is used in the wall hanging is double the size of the brolga on the cushion.

The heavy lines show the design motif outline. The dotted lines indicate the underlap for the pieces, where needed. The fine lines are suggested embroidery lines.

## *Decorative bookmarks*

Use small motifs to make bookmarks. The small size is suitable for a paperback novel, the larger size for a hardback book. The bookmarks are shown in colour facing page 16.

Flowers can also be drawn in reverse to vary shape

### Materials
**Small size**
- 8 cm x 23 cm (3 in x 9 in) fabric for front
- 8 cm x 23 cm (3 in x 9 in) fabric for lining

**Large size**
- 8 cm x 32 cm (3 in x 13 in) fabric for front
- 8 cm x 32 cm (3 in x 13 in) fabric for lining
- Vliesofix®
- scraps of fabric for appliqués
- Tearaway®
- tassel (optional)

### Method
1 Following the instructions for Vliesofix® on page 6, trace and apply the design to the appliqué fabric. Cut out the pieces.
2 Arrange the pieces on the background fabric.
3 Iron on Tearaway® backing.
4 Satin stitch the edges of the appliqués.
5 Machine or hand embroider the details (see Embroidery on page 9).
6 Tear away backing.
7 Pin the lining to the bookmark with the right sides together. Mark the stitching line along the sides and around the bottom point (see diagram). Stitch, leaving an opening of about 4 cm (1¹/2 in)  on one side so that you can turn the piece.

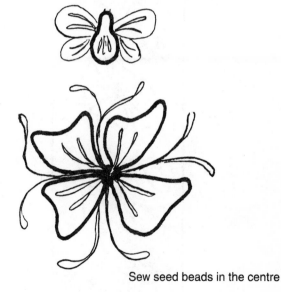

Sew seed beads in the centre

For butterfly motif, see page 28

17

**8** Trim the corners close to the stitching.
**9** Turn so that the right side is out.
**10** Press, making sure all edges are straight.
**11** Slip stitch the opening together.
**12** Top stitch 6 mm (¼ in) from the edge.
**13** Sew on the tassel to finish it.

# Floral glasses case

This project uses the same motifs as the bookmark, but the flowers are arranged all over the case. The glasses case is shown in colour facing page 16.

## Materials

- 19 cm x 25 cm (7½ in x 10 in) fabric
- 19 cm x 25 cm (7½ in x 10 in) lining
- 19 cm x 25 cm (7½ in x 10 in) Pellon or lightweight batting
- scraps of fabric for appliqués
- Vliesofix®
- Tearaway®
- 75 cm x 4 cm (30 in x 1½ in) background fabric cut on the bias
- 8 cm x 3 cm (3 in x 1¼ in) bias strip for button loop

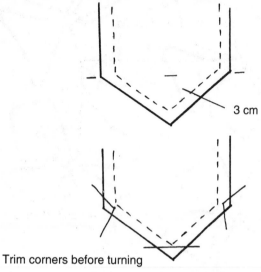

Trim corners before turning

Placement for book mark

Placement for glasses case

- 19-mm (³/₄-in) button OR use a button covering kit
- Seed beads for flower centres

## Method

1 Following the instructions for Vliesofix® on page 6, trace and apply the design to the appliqué fabric. Cut out the pieces.
2 Place the motifs on the background fabric, arranging them so that the design can be seen on the front fold-over flap and there is a space for a button on the bottom fold-up section (see diagram for suggested placement).
3 Iron on Tearaway® backing.
4 Satin stitch around the flowers and bees.
5 Machine or hand embroider the bees' wings and the stamens on the flowers (see Embroidery on page 9).
6 Stitch beads in place.
7 Tear away backing.
8 Sandwich the Pellon between the lining and the appliqué piece with the wrong sides against the Pellon.
9 Pin the layers together, making sure everything is straight and smooth (see Quilting by machine on page 12).
10 Mark the quilting lines (see diagram).
11 Using Monofil or a matching thread, stitch over the lines.
12 Fold the longer bias strip in half and using a 6-mm (¹/₄-in) seam allowance, stitch it across right side of the bottom edge keeping all the raw edges together.
13 Turn the bias strip over the raw edges, and slip stitch it in place.
14 Round the corners of the top flap. Mark 2 cm (³/₄ in) in each direction from the corners, mark curve and cut to shape (see diagram).
15 Make a rouleau button loop from the small bias strip. Fold it in half with the right sides together and stitch 6 mm (¹/₄ in) from the edge. Turn to the right side and press with the seam to one side, then fold with the seam on the inner edge and the ends even (see diagram). Press.
16 Baste the loop to the centre of flap along the stitching line. Make sure the loop is just big enough to slip over the button. Trim away any excess fabric.
17 Fold the bottom up 8 cm (3 in) and pin it in place.
18 Using a 6-mm (¹/₄-in) seam, stitch the rest of the bias fabric to right side of glasses case, turning the raw edges under at the beginning and end and easing it around the corners.

19 Fold bias over to cover the raw edges, and slip stitch it in place.
20 Stitch on the button.

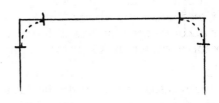

Round corners of top flap

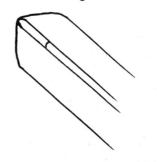

Folding rouleau for button fastening

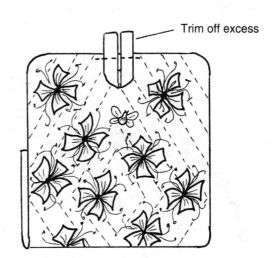

Trim off excess

Quilting lines

## FLORAL GLASSES CASE

# Jewelled Fan box top

This is a novel way to decorate a box lid. It can be as ornate or simple as you want. The wooden box illustrated is 20 cm x 15 cm (8 in x 6 in) with a lid inset of 16.5 cm x 11.5 cm (6½ in x 4½ in).

The fan appliqué consists of two simple shapes. The outer one can be straight or scalloped. This same design could be used on blocks for a patchwork quilt, and you could alternate the colours of the fans or decorate each fan in a different way.

The box top is shown in colour facing page 16.

## Materials
- box with a recessed panel in the lid (available from craft and embroidery supply shops)
- 2 pieces of toning or contrasting fabric for appliqué
- fabric for background, it should be 5 cm (2 in) larger all around than the insert on the box lid
- Vliesofix®
- Tearaway®
- fabric for lining
- 1 or 2 pieces of batting (depending on how padded you want the lid) slightly larger than the insert on the box lid
- beads, jewels and threads to decorate

## Method
1 Following the instructions for Vliesofix® on page 6, trace and apply the fan to the appliqué fabric. Cut out the pieces.

2 Arrange the pieces on the background fabric.
3 Iron on Tearaway® backing.
4 Satin stitch around the appliqué shapes.
5 Decorate the fan with a combination of embroidery, beads and jewels, which have been stitched or glued on.
6 Remove Tearaway® backing.
7 Place the batting on top of the box insert and stretch the appliquéd piece smoothly over the top. Lace it to the top of the box working both from top to bottom and from side to side, to hold it firmly in place (see diagram). Cut away

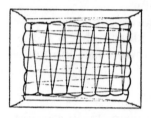

Lace the appliquéd panel over the lid/insert

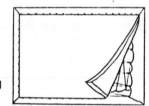

Stitch lining over the lacing

any unnecessary bulk at the corners.

8 Cut a piece of lining fabric the same size as the box insert. Turn under 6 mm (¼ in) along all the edges and slip stitch the lining into place.
9 Clip the finished appliqué into the recessed panel on the box lid.

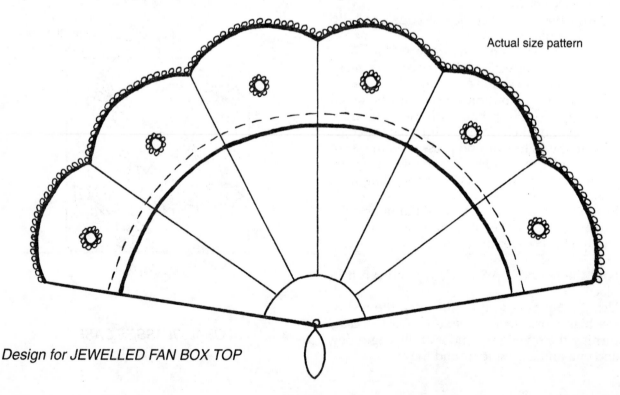

*Design for JEWELLED FAN BOX TOP*

Actual size pattern

# *Lazy Days library bag*

Schools or kindergartens often ask for a library bag to keep children's books safe and clean while being carried. Here is an appropriate design to brighten such a bag.

The bag is shown in colour on the centre spread.

## Materials

- 78 cm x 60 cm (31 in x 24 in) fabric for bag
- small pieces of fabric for appliqués
- Vliesofix®
- Tearaway®
- embellishments: have a variety of bits and pieces such as lace flowers, small pieces of ribbon for neck ties, ladybird buttons, novelty ribbon for hat feathers, etc.
- eyes: 1 x 6-mm (1/4-in), 1 x 12-mm (1/2-in); they can be the glue-on or stitch on variety
- 1 m (1 yd) of piping cord for drawstring

*Design for LAZY DAYS LIBRARY BAG*

## Method

1 Following the instructions for Vliesofix® on page 6, trace and apply the design to the appliqué fabric. Cut out the pieces.
2 Arrange the pieces on the background fabric.
3 Iron on Tearaway® backing.

Embroider stems and attach lace flowers

Embroider hat bands and library bag tie

Actual size pattern

Neck ties are ribbons

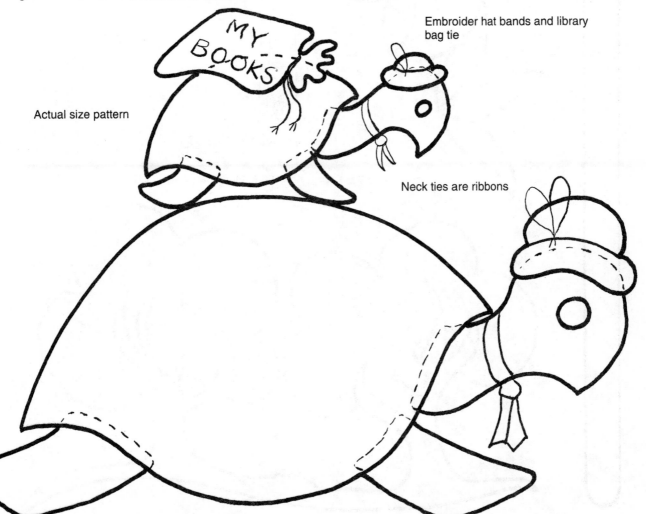

**4** Satin stitch around the edges of the appliqués.

**5** Stitch on flowers, ribbons and any other embellishments.

**6** Tear away backing.

**7** Make up the bag using French seams. To do this, stitch the seams with the wrong sides together first, then turn the bag inside out and stitch the seams with the right sides together so that the first seams are enclosed.

**8** On either side of the seam, make 1.5-cm (⁵⁄₈-in) buttonholes 7 cm (2³⁄₄ in) down from the top of the bag.

**9** Fold the top 6 cm (2¹⁄₂ in) over to the inside, and hem it in place.

**10** Top stitch around the top edge of the bag.

**11** Thread the cord through the buttonholes and knot the ends.

Actual size pattern

Placement for library bag

# Owls at Sea overalls

These patterns can be used in many ways and different combinations, depending on the style of the overalls. For example, the windsurfing owl or the owls in a boat could be used alone on a bib front, or the fish could decorate the patch pockets.

To begin, you will need to cut out the overalls, but do not make them up until the appliqué is completed. The only exception to this is if an appliqué crosses a seam line such as the centre-front seam in the overalls photographed on the

centre spread. Be careful to place the appliqués away from seam lines to be stitched later.

## Materials
- purchased overalls pattern
- fabric and notions specified by the pattern
- small pieces of fabric for appliqués
- Vliesofix®
- Tearaway®
- eyes. I used 5-mm, 8-mm and 10-mm ($\frac{1}{4}$–$\frac{3}{8}$ in); they can be the glue-on or stitch-on variety (if you use glue-on eyes, you will need a

*Design for OWLS AT SEA OVERALLS*

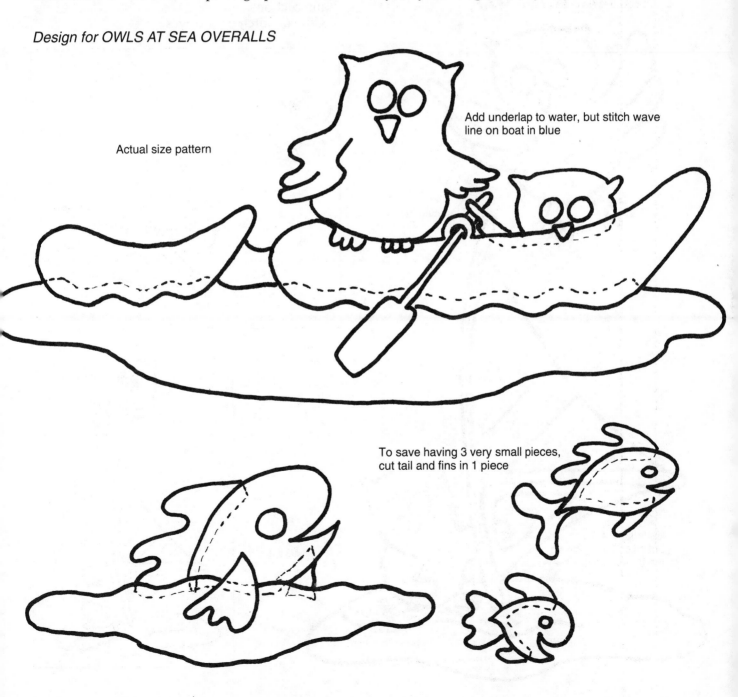

Actual size pattern

Add underlap to water, but stitch wave line on boat in blue

To save having 3 very small pieces, cut tail and fins in 1 piece

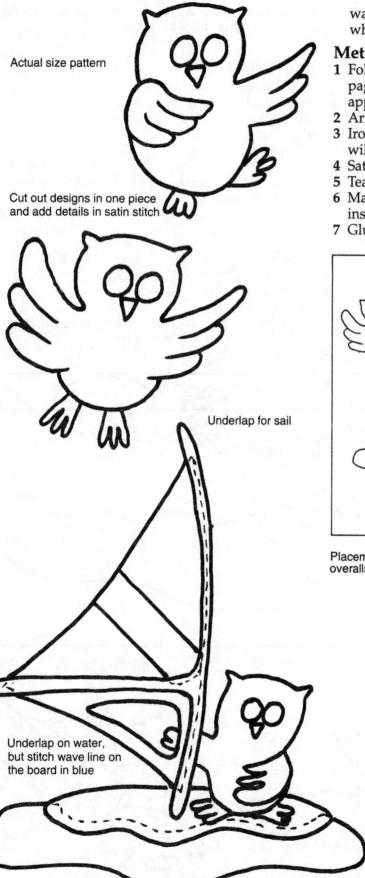

Actual size pattern

Cut out designs in one piece
and add details in satin stitch

Underlap for sail

Underlap on water,
but stitch wave line on
the board in blue

washable glue such as Helmar Gemstone glue,
which is available from craft stores)

## Method

1 Following the instructions for Vliesofix® on
page 6, trace and apply the design to the
appliqué fabric. Cut out the pieces.
2 Arrange the pieces on the overall pieces.
3 Iron on the Tearaway® backing to the areas that
will have appliqués.
4 Satin stitch around the edges of the appliqués.
5 Tear away backing.
6 Make up the overalls according to pattern
instructions.
7 Glue or stitch on the eyes.

Placement for
overalls

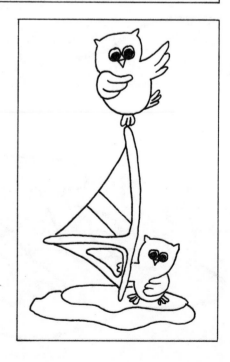

# Fish at Play hat

There are many commercial hat patterns available to choose from. Appliqués can be placed on the brim or crown, depending on the style of hat. Having chosen a hat pattern, cut out the pieces but do not make up the hat until all the appliqué is complete. The hat shown in colour on the centre spread has four pieces for the crown, so four different fish were used. Be careful to place appliqués away from the seam lines.

## Materials
- purchased hat pattern
- fabric and notions as specified by the pattern
- small pieces of fabric for appliqués
- Vliesofix®

- Tearaway®
- eyes. I used 8-mm (³/8-in); they can be the glue-on or stitch-on variety (if you use glue-on eyes, you will need a washable glue such as Helmar Gemstone glue, which is available from craft stores)

## Method
1 Following the instructions for Vliesofix® on page 6, trace and apply the design to the appliqué fabric. Cut out the pieces.
2 Arrange the appliqués on the hat pieces.
3 Iron on Tearaway® backing to the areas that will have appliqués.
4 Satin stitch around the edges of the appliqués.
5 Tear away backing and make up the hat according to pattern instructions.
6 Glue or stitch on the eyes.

*Design for FISH AT PLAY HAT*

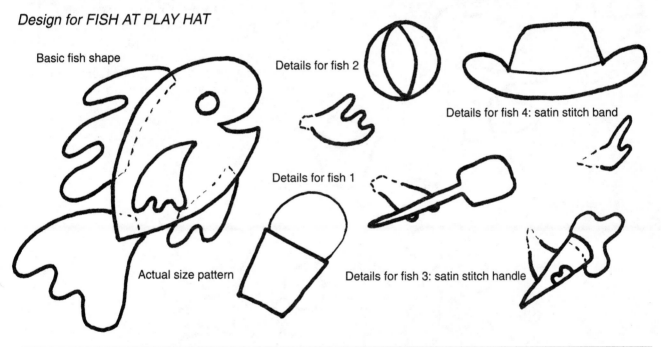

Basic fish shape

Details for fish 2

Details for fish 4: satin stitch band

Details for fish 1

Actual size pattern

Details for fish 3: satin stitch handle

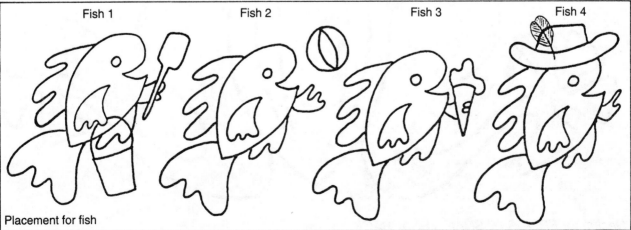

Fish 1   Fish 2   Fish 3   Fish 4

Placement for fish

# Frogs 'n Snails knapsack

Appliqués can be used to decorate bags in any style from simple carry bags through to more complicated knapsacks with a variety of pockets and flaps. Choose a bag pattern that has flaps, pockets or flat areas that can be easily decorated. This child's knapsack was made from McCalls pattern 6752.

The knapsack is shown in colour on the centre spread.

## Materials
- purchased bag pattern
- fabric, lining and notions as specified by the pattern
- small pieces of fabric for appliqués
- Vliesofix®
- Tearaway® or iron-on Vilene® (see note)
- eyes: I used 8-mm and 10-mm (approximately $^3/_8$ in), they can be the glue-on or stick-on variety (if you use glue-on eyes, you will need a washable glue such as Helmar Gemstone glue, which is available from craft stores)

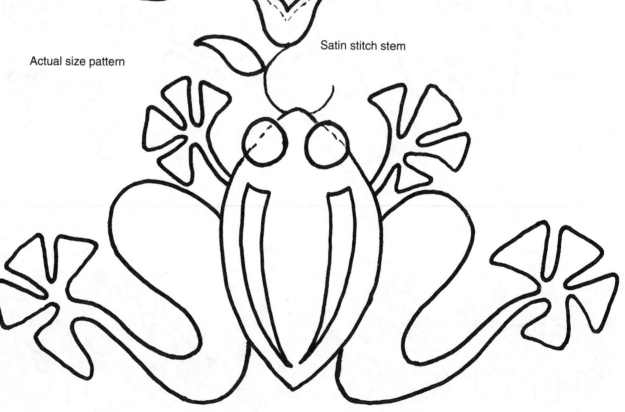

Actual size pattern

Satin stitch stem

*Design for FROGS 'N' SNAILS KNAPSACK*

## Method

1 Begin by cutting out all the pieces of the knapsack and decide where you want the appliqués.
2 Following the instructions for Vliesofix® on page 6, trace and apply the design to the appliqué fabric. Cut out the pieces.

> **Note:** If you are putting an appliqué on a flap, for example, which needs interfacing, you can use iron-on Vilene® interfacing to stabilise the appliqué and leave it there instead of using Tearaway®.

3 Arrange the appliqués on the knapsack pieces, which have been stabilised. The shapes should be applied before the bag construction begins. Make sure the appliqués do not go over any seam lines.
4 Satin stitch around the edges of the appliqués.
5 The snail shell lines are also worked in satin stitch. This can be done as part of the machine appliqué, hand embroidered in stem stitch or just left plain.
6 Machine or hand embroider snail trail lines, eyes, mouths and feelers (see Embroidery on page 9).
7 Tear away backing.
8 Make up bag.
9 Glue or stitch on eyes.

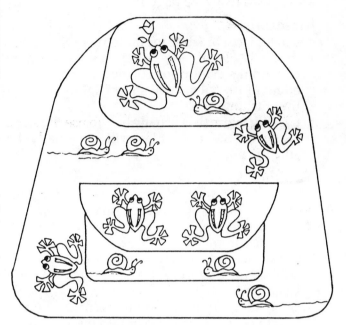

Placement for knapsack

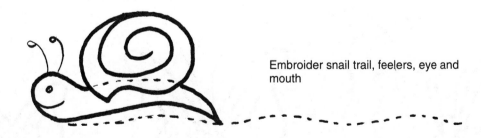

Embroider snail trail, feelers, eye and mouth

Actual size pattern

# 3D Butterflies

These butterflies are easy to make and can be used on many different articles of clothing or greetings cards. The technique can also be used for other flying creatures or to make life-like flowers.

The butterflies are shown in colour on the Blue Meadow Mats facing page 16.

## Materials
- small pieces of fabric for butterflies
- iron-on Vilene®; use black, white or grey depending on the colour of the butterflies as the edges of the Vilene will show slightly through the stitching.
- backing fabric (it is usually best to use the same fabric as the butterflies will eventually be stitched to).

## Method
1 Trace the butterfly designs on Vliesofix®, cut out the motifs leaving a small margin all around, then apply to the wrong side of the butterfly fabric and cut out.
2 Cut a piece of backing fabric large enough to hold all the butterflies, plus 2.5 cm (1 in) extra all around.
3 Depending on how firm you want the butterflies to be, cut either one or two pieces of iron-on Vilene the same size as the backing.

4 Lay backing with the right side facing down and fuse the one or two layers of iron-on Vilene to it.
5 Peel away the Vliesofix® backing from the butterflies and arrange them on the prepared backing. Fuse the layers together.
6 Satin stitch around the edges of the butterflies.
7 Complete any machine or hand embroidery or beading on the butterflies.
8 Cut out butterflies being **very** careful not to cut the satin-stitched threads.

> **Note:** If you do snip a thread accidentally, a tiny drop of craft glue on the end of a toothpick will hold the stitch down and the glue will dry clear. If the edges of the iron-on Vilene are too visible, they can be carefully coloured with fabric pens or even ordinary felt tipped pens if the article is not going to be washed.

## Butterfly bodies
The butterfly is attached to the background fabric by its body. This can either be satin stitched or made from fabric.

### Making and attaching a fabric body
1 Trace the body on Vliesofix® and cut it out, leaving a small margin all around. Iron the Vliesofix® to the wrong side of the body fabric and cut it out.

Actual size pattern

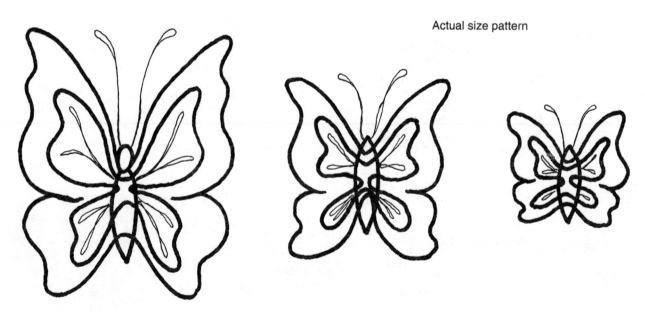

*Design for 3D BUTTERFLIES*

**2** Place the butterfly wings in position on the background fabric and hold in place with pins.

**3** Peel the Vliesofix® backing from body and, using the tip of the iron, fuse the body in place.

**4** Iron a piece of Tearaway® on the back of the work to stabilise the fabric where you will stitch.

**5** Begin satin stitching from behind the head and continue all the way around.

**6** Machine or hand embroider the feelers on the background (see Embroidery on page 9).

### Attaching the butterfly with satin stitch

**1** Position the butterfly wings as in 2 above and use a piece of Tearaway® on the back of your work to stabilise the fabric.

**2** Satin stitch the body by beginning at the top of the head with two or three stitches in one place

to anchor the thread. Increase then decrease the zigzag stitch smoothly and quickly, making a circle for the head. Increase again, graduating the zigzag stitch so that the widest part of the body is just before the centre of the wings, then gradually decreasing the zigzag width to 0 at the end of the body.

**3** Fasten off either with small stitches or pull the top thread to the back and knot. Increase again, graduating the zigzag stitch so that the widest part of the body is just before the centre of the wings, then gradually decreasing the zigzag width to 0 at the end of the body.

**4** Machine or hand embroider feelers on the background (see Embroidery on page 9).

Butterflies ready for stitching

A = backing
B, C = iron-on Vilene

# Blue Meadow place mats and serviette rings

These place mats and serviette rings are quite eye-catching for a special occasion, especially if they are made in colours to tone with your dinner setting. They are photographed in colour facing page 16.

## Place mats

The finished mat size is 38 cm x 28 cm (15 in x 11 in) without the frill.

### Materials

- 2 pieces of fabric each 30 cm x 40 cm (12 in x 16 in) for each mat
- 1 3D butterfly for each mat (see page 28)

> **Note:** 1.7 m of fabric would be ample for six mats and six serviette rings. However, if you want ruffles on the mats you will need extra fabric, this should be 8 cm (3 in) wide by twice the length of the finished ruffle.

- small pieces of fabric for appliqués
- seed beads for the flower centres (optional)
- Vliesofix®
- Tearaway®

## Method

1. Make one 8-cm (3-in) 3D butterfly for each mat.
2. Follow the instructions for Vliesofix® on page 6, trace and apply the flowers and leaves to the fabric. Cut out the pieces.
3. Arrange the pieces on the mats, which have been backed with Tearaway® stabiliser, as shown in the diagram.
4. Satin stitch around the edges of the appliqués.
5. Attach the 3D butterfly to the top left hand corner (keep it away from the seam lines), using either a fabric or satin-stitched body.
6. Complete the machine or hand embroidery and sew on beads.
7. Remove Tearaway® backing.
8. If no ruffle is required, place the mat and lining with the right sides together and stitch around the edge with a 6-mm (1/4-in) seam allowance, leaving an opening on one side big enough to turn the mat through. Trim the corners. Turn the mat to the right side, making sure the corners are neatly turned. Slip stitch the opening together and press the mat. Finish by top stitching with a matching or contrasting thread 6 mm (1/4 in) from the edge.
9. For instructions on making ruffles see Cushions on page 41.

Actual size pattern

*Design for FLOWERS and PLACEMATS*

30

# Serviette rings

## Materials
- 2 pieces of fabric each 6.5 cm x 18 cm (2½ in x 7 in) for each serviette ring
- 1 3D butterfly for each serviette ring (see page 28)
- Small strip of Velcro for fasteners

## Method
1 For each serviette ring make one 5-cm (2-in) 3D butterfly.
2 Apply 3D butterfly to the centre of the serviette ring fabric so that it will be flying towards the mat, and sew with either a fabric or satin-stitched body.
3 Embroider the feelers.
4 Place the serviette ring and lining with the right sides together and stitch around, leaving a 5-cm (2-in) opening to turn the piece through.

> **Note:** Because the 3D butterfly wings reach beyond the seam line you will have to stitch up to the wing, lift the presser foot and move the work, then continue on the other side.

5 Turn the work through the 5-cm (2-in) opening and slip stitch the opening closed. Also slip stitch the small gaps under the wings.
6 Machine the fluffy side of a small strip of Velcro to the end of the lining, and the matching grip side of the Velcro to the top.

Placement for place mats

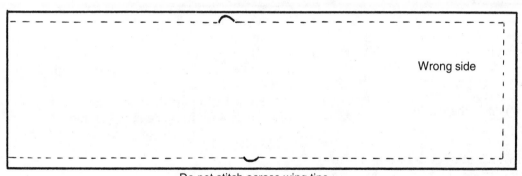

Wrong side

Do not stitch across wing tips

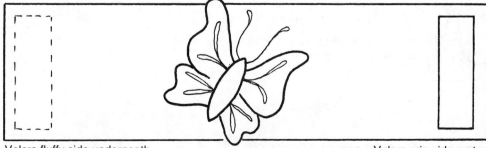

Velcro fluffy side underneath

Velcro grip side on top

# Butterfly hair combs

The butterflies for these hair combs were made using a slight variation on the 3D-butterfly method. As there is no background fabric to attach these to, the fabric bodies were stitched to the wings before the whole butterflies were cut out.

The combs are shown in colour facing page 32.

## Materials
• plain purchased hair combs
• 3 small 3D butterflies to fit across each hair comb (see page 28)

## Method
1 Make the 3.5-cm (1¼-in) 3D butterflies following the first six steps of the instructions on page 28.
2 Trace the bodies on Vliesofix®.
3 Cut out the Vliesofix® for the bodies, leaving a margin around the edge and fuse to the back of the body fabric.
4 Cut out the bodies accurately.
5 Peel off the Vliesofix® backing and fuse the bodies in place over the satin-stitched butterfly wings.
6 Beginning at a point, satin stitch around the body.
7 Complete any machine or hand embroidery or beading.
8 Cut out butterflies being very careful not to cut the satin-stitched threads.

> **Note:** If you do snip a thread accidentally, a tiny drop of craft glue on the end of a toothpick will hold the stitch down and the glue will dry clear. If edges of the iron-on Vilene are too visible, they can be carefully coloured with fabric pens or even ordinary felt tipped pens if the article is not going to be washed.

9 Using a double thread, stitch the butterflies to the combs, spacing them evenly and making sure the securing thread does not show on the front.

> **Note:** On most combs, attaching the butterflies either side of the centre prong and either side of the third prong in from each end will work well.

# Butterfly picture

Small pictures can be made with one or more butterflies. You could appliqué or embroider flowers around them or apply the butterflies to a patterned background for a pretty effect.

A butterfly picture is shown in colour facing page 16.

## Materials
• 3D butterflies, as many as you want (see page 28)
• purchased picture frame; the picture illustrated was made using a 12-cm (5-in) frame with a 9.5-cm (3¾-in) plastic insert to stretch the fabric across (available from embroidery supply stores)
• fabric for background; allow yourself enough fabric to turn under the insert
• craft glue

## Method
1 Make the 3D butterflies following the first six steps of the instructions on page 28.
2 Attach the completed butterflies to the background fabric, adding any embroidery you desire.

> **Note:** Make sure your design will fit in the picture frame, although the edge of the fabric should extend approximately 2.5 cm (1 in) past the plastic insert.

3 When your design is complete, run a gathering stitch around the edge of the background fabric.
4 Place the insert underneath your design, pull up the gathering thread and secure with a few stitches.
5 A little craft glue applied to the back of your work will hold it in place in the frame.

*A distinctive and co-ordinated look for clothes and accessories. The* Autumn
Flowers Vest *and* Belt *worn with the* Butterfly Hair Combs.
*The photograph on the back cover shows the front view of the vest and belt.*

*The* Tree of Life Wall Hanging *is stunning, but the design could also be
simplified and used for a cushion, or made into a quilt. Greetings cards can be
made using any small motifs.*

*A collection of appliquéd items to delight any child: the* Owl and the Pussycat Wall Hanging, Lazy Days Library Bag, Fish at Play Hat *and* Owls at Sea Overalls. *The motifs on the overalls and hat are adapted from those used for the wall hanging. They could also be used on a T-shirt or jacket.*

INSET: *The* Kite Cot Quilt *is made from brightly coloured fabrics. Make more or fewer kites so that you can spell out the child's name across the quilt.*

*Two wall hangings for the nursery:* Frogs Down by the Pond *and*
Tortoises. *These designs have been adapted for the* Lazy Days *library bag
and the* Frogs 'n' Snails Knapsack *shown above. Another variation on the
owl theme has been added to the back of the overalls, while the hat features*
Fish at Play.

LEFT: *This* **Summer Garland Jacket** *includes three-dimensional butterflies.*
RIGHT: *The* **Pheasants and Flowers Jacket** *won first prize at the Australasian Quilters' Symposium in 1990.*

*Both jackets are hand beaded and you could make a matching skirt or blouse using your favourite fabric from the appliqués.*

# Greetings cards

You can make personalised cards for special occasions. Use 3D butterflies or flowers or, for children's cards, frogs, snails or whatever is appropriate.

Either use a purchased card that is designed for embroidery inserts or make your own by the following method. Instructions are for a card 13 cm x 20 cm (5 in x 8 in).

A card is shown illustrated in colour facing page 32.

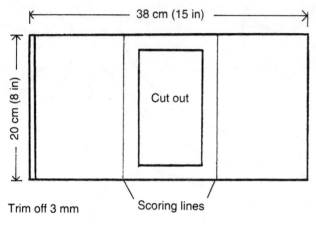

Trim off 3 mm      Scoring lines

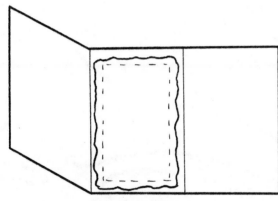

Back of appliqué

Children's cards: *use any of the motifs which will appeal to children to make a special greeting card. It can then be framed as a keepsake.*

## Materials

- 10 cm x 18 cm (4 in x 7 in) background fabric
- small pieces of fabric for appliqués
- Vliesofix®
- Tearaway®
- 20 cm x 38 cm (8 in x 15 in) strong paper or thin card
- craft knife
- metal edged ruler
- fabric and paper glue

## Method

1 Make up an appliquéd panel 8 cm x 15 cm (3 in x 6 in) with an extra 12 mm (½ in) of fabric all around.
2 Mark the piece of card into thirds along both 38 cm (15 in) sides and carefully score between the markings so that the card will fold easily.
3 In the centre third, mark out a rectangle 2.5 cm (1 in) in from all sides. Cut out the centre using the ruler and craft knife.
4 Trim 3 mm (⅛ in) from the outside left-hand edge of the card.
5 Turn the card to the right side and rule a gold or coloured line 6 mm (¼ in) from the cut edges of the centre rectangle.
6 Apply glue around the inside of the centre frame and press the appliqué carefully into place.
7 Glue the left flap of the card and press into place, covering the back of the appliqué.

Frogs can be cut all in one piece or, for more flexibility with the arrangement, cut the body and legs separately with a generous underlap

# Nursery wall hangings

Here are some ideas for brightening up a nursery wall. They are effective either left as simple shapes with basic stitching or embellished with beads, sequins, ribbons or whatever you have at hand.

The Frog panel and the Tortoise hanging are shown in the centre spread.

Actual size pattern

# Frogs down by the Pond wall hanging

Finished measurement is approximately 62 cm (24 in) square.

## Materials

- 55-cm (21-in) square of fabric for background
- 60 cm (24 in) of 115-cm (45-in) fabric for appliqués and borders
- fabric scraps for appliqué highlights
- 65-cm (26-in) square of backing fabric
- 65-cm (26-in) square of Pellon or light-weight batting
- Vliesofix®
- Tearaway®
- beads and sequins for trims

## Method

1 Following the instructions for Vliesofix® on page 6, trace and apply the frogs and dragon-fly shapes to the appliqué fabric. Cut out the pieces.
2 Arrange the appliqués on the background using the photograph as a guide to placement.
3 Iron on the Tearaway® backing.
4 Satin stitch all around the appliqués and embellish with beads, sequins, etc.
5 Remove the Tearaway® backing.
6 To make the borders, cut four strips the length of the sides x 5 cm (2 in). Cut four corner blocks 5 cm x 5 cm (2 in x 2 in). Join one border to the top and one to the bottom. Join the corner blocks to each end of the remaining two borders. Attach these borders to the sides, matching the corner blocks exactly. They will fit snugly into place if you press the already joined seams in opposite directions (see diagram).
7 Assemble as instructed in Quilting by machine on page 12, then bind the edges of the hanging (see page 15).

*Design for DRAGON FLY for WALL HANGING*

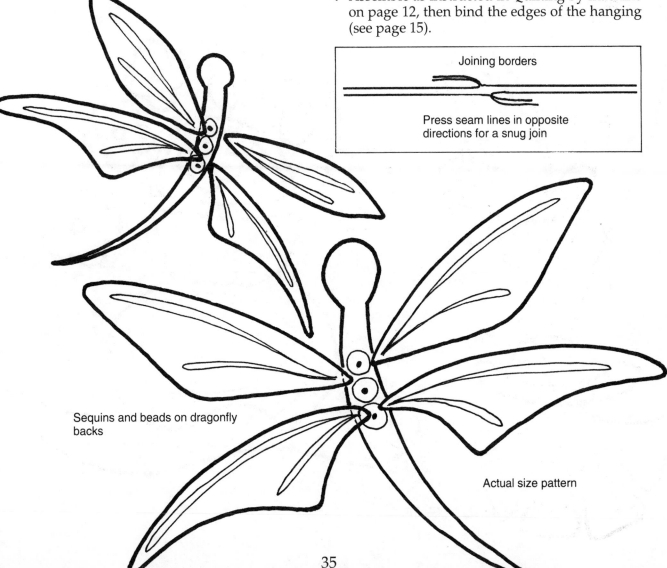

Joining borders

Press seam lines in opposite directions for a snug join

Sequins and beads on dragonfly backs

Actual size pattern

# Tortoise wall hanging

The wall hanging illustrated is 61 cm (24 in) square and is divided into three sections.

## Materials

- 56-cm (22-in) square of fabric for background
- 65 cm (26 in) of 115-cm (45-in) contrasting fabric for appliqués and borders
- fabric scraps for heads, feet, butterflies and other small details
- Vliesofix®
- Tearaway®
- 65-cm (26-in) square of Pellon or light-weight batting
- beads, sequins, lace and ribbons for trims

## Method

1 Construct the background following the diagram. Add 5-cm (2-in) borders. The corners can be either mitred or square.
2 Following the instructions for Vliesofix® on page 6, trace and apply the design to the appliqué fabric. Cut out the pieces.

3 Arrange the appliqués on the background using the photograph as a guide to placement of the pieces.
4 Iron on the Tearaway® backing.
5 Satin stitch around the appliqués.
6 Embroider the butterfly details and flower stems by hand or machine.
7 The lace on the hat can be satin stitched on with the appliquéd hat piece.
8 Beads can be stitched in swirls to suggest the tortoise and snail shells.
9 The necklaces on the tortoises are strings of beads attached at either end with the middle hanging free.
10 Remove Tearaway® backing.
11 When all embellishing is completed, put the quilt top, batting and backing together and quilt (see Quilting by machine on page 12).
12 Bind the edge of the hanging following the instructions on page 15.

Actual size pattern

*Design for TORTOISE WALL HANGING*

Pieced background

Add seam allowances

15 cm (6 in)

15 cm (6 in)

15 cm (6 in)

12 mm (½ in)

12 mm (½ in)

51 cm (20 in)

Actual size pattern

*Note:* Also use tortoise from library bag, page 21

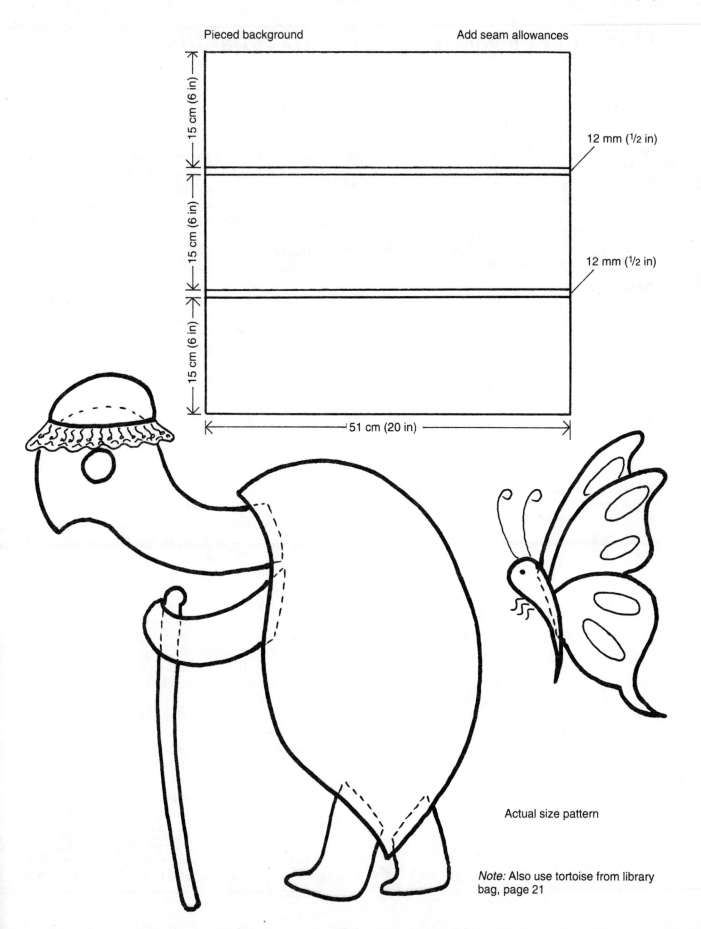

# Owls and Pussycats wall hanging

If you can find fabrics that have either a single motif or repeated motifs suitable for appliquéing, then you can use that fabric as the basis for a picture as has been done with the cats in this wall hanging. Instead of drawing your design on Vliesofix®, first decide which part of the fabric you want to use, then cut a piece of Vliesofix® that will cover the design (in this case a group of cats) leaving a margin of Vliesofix® all around.

This project is shown in colour on the front cover and on the centre spread.

## Materials
- printed fabrics
- background and other fabrics, depending on the design
- backing fabric
- Pellon or light-weight batting
- Vliesofix®
- Tearaway®

## Method
1 Iron the Vliesofix® on the back of the printed fabric.
2 Cut out the design.
3 Peel the paper backing away and iron your design on the background fabric along with all the other pieces for your picture or wall hanging.
4 Proceed as usual for the appliqué using a narrow satin stitch around the printed design so as not to obscure too much of the print.
5 Make up your wall hanging following the instructions for Quilting by machine (page 12) and Finishing a quilt (page 15).

# Kite cot quilt

This cot quilt is a good opportunity to use up brightly coloured pieces of fabric in the kites and borders. The finished size of the Kite cot quilt is approximately 101 cm x 140 cm (40 in x 55 in) and it is shown in colour on the centre spread.

The rectangular shaped kites vary in size from 20 cm x 12.5 cm (8 in x 5 in) to 27 cm x 15 cm (10½ in x 6 in) and they could have straight or slightly concave sides. To personalise the quilt, appliqué the child's name, one letter on each kite.

## Materials
- 70 cm x 102 cm (27 in x 40 in) of fabric for central panel
- 1.5 m (60 in) fabric in total for borders, select contrasting colours for maximum effect
- small pieces of fabric for appliquéd kites, kite tails, bears and trees
- 115 cm x 152 cm (45 in x 60 in) backing fabric
- 115 cm x 152 cm (45 in x 60 in) light-weight batting
- Vliesofix®
- Tearaway®
- 6 m (6½ yd) of 2-mm or 3-mm (⅛-in) ribbons in different colours

## Method
1 Following the instructions for Vliesofix® on page 6, trace and apply the shapes to the appliqué fabric. Cut out the pieces. If you are using letters for a child's name, draw out block letters to fit into a shape approximately 4–5 cm (1½–2 in) square. Remember to trace the letters on the Vliesofix® in reverse.
2 Arrange the pieces on the background, including the four corner bear blocks.
3 Iron on Tearaway® backing.
4 Satin stitch around the appliqués, including the ribbons as you stitch the kite shapes (see 5 and 6 below).
5 For the ribbons on the kites, cut the ribbons into 10-cm (4-in) lengths and use three lengths for each side of the kites. Pin the ribbons across the edges of your appliqué so that as you satin stitch around the kites the ends of the ribbons are stitched firmly in place. Cut off any excess ribbon ends after sewing them in place.
6 For the ribbons on the kite tails, cut the ribbons into 4-cm (1½-in) lengths and, using two pieces, pin in place so they form a cross over the stitching line of the kite's tail. Satin stitch the tail.

*Design for KITE COT QUILT*
80% actual size

Kite strings are quilting lines

Ribbons held in place
with satin stitch

7  Embroider the details. Use French knots for the bears' eyes and nose details.
8  Remove Tearaway® backing.
9  Assemble the quilt top and borders following the diagram.
10  Baste or pin the top, batting and backing together.
11  Hand or machine quilt. Use outline quilting for the kites, bears and trees. Use quilting lines to suggest kite strings and clouds. Quilt in the ditch around the centre panel and borders and, if desired, free-machine quilt over the borders also.
12  Bring the backing over to the front and slip stitch into place to bind the edge of the quilt.

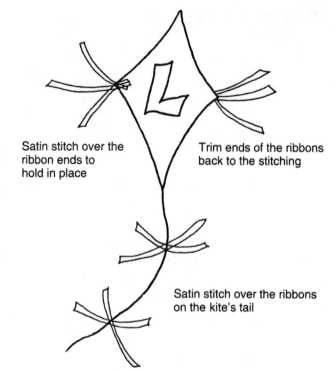

Satin stitch over the ribbon ends to hold in place

Trim ends of the ribbons back to the stitching

Satin stitch over the ribbons on the kite's tail

Corner of Kite cot quilt showing borders

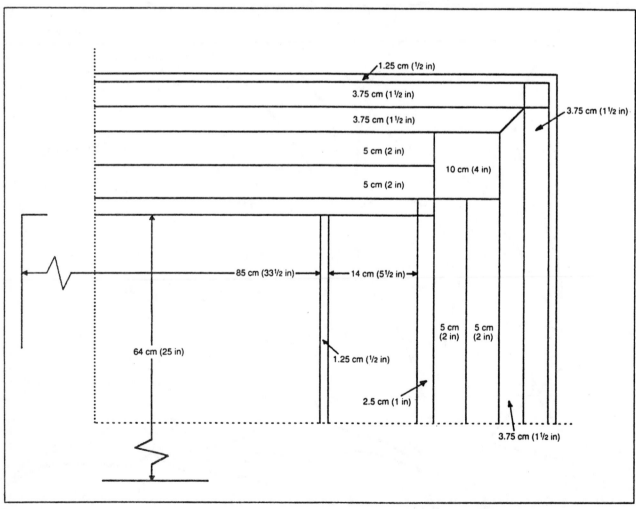

# Gum Blossom cushions

Each finished cushion is 46 cm (18 in) square, but could easily be made larger or smaller depending on how you arrange the gum blossoms and leaves. The cushion can be finished with either a piped edge or a frill.

The cushion is shown in colour facing page 17.

## Materials

- 2 51-cm (20-in) squares of fabric for back and front of cushion
- 51-cm (20-in) square of Pellon and the same size piece of a light-weight fabric, such as lawn, if you want to quilt the top
- small pieces of green and brown fabric for appliqués
- 40-cm (16-in) zipper
- size 20 (50 cm or 20 in) cushion insert
- Vliesofix®
- Tearaway®
- red seed beads
- 4.25 m x 9 cm (4¹/2 yd x 3¹/4 in) fabric for a gathered frill OR
- 1 m (1 yd) of piping cord and a piece of fabric 1 m x 4 cm (1 yd x 1¹/2 in) for a piped edge

## Method

1 Following the instructions for Vliesofix® on page 6, trace the leaves and branches and apply the appliqué fabric. Cut out the pieces.
2 Arrange the appliqués on the fabric for the cushion top, leaving one or two gaps to fill with embroidered gum blossoms.
3 Iron on Tearaway® backing.
4 Complete all the satin stitching on the leaves and branches.
5 Mark the position of the gum blossom centres.
6 With your machine set for free machining, complete the gum blossoms (see Embroidery by machine on page 10).
7 Sew the seed beads at intervals around the edges of the blossoms to highlight them.
8 Remove Tearaway® backing.
9 If desired, quilt the top (see Quilting by machine on page 12).
10 Make up the cushion following the instructions below.

## Making up a cushion

1 The completed top should be 48-cm (19-in) square. Round off the corners.
2 Cut a back 48 cm x 51 cm (19 in x 19¹/2 in). Round off the corners.

3 Measure 10 cm (4 in) down on the 51-cm (19¹/2-in) side and cut the material into two pieces at that point (the cut runs between the long sides). This forms the zipper opening.
4 Pin and stitch the back pieces approximately 4 cm (1¹/2 in) from each end to form an enclosed opening for the zipper.
5 Trim and neaten the seam.
6 Stitch in the zipper.

### Ruffles

Use this section if trimming a cushion or place mat with a ruffle.

1 Cut the fabric 8 cm (3 in) wide by twice the length of the sides of the cushion.
2 Fold the 8-cm (3-in) strip exactly in half lengthways and press. Using a gathering thread or the ruffle attachment on your machine, gather the fabric up to half its length.
3 Round the corners on the cushion or mat and lining.
4 Baste the ruffle to the right side of the cushion or mat top, easing it around the corners. Turn the raw edges of the ruffle on each end to the inside.
5 Place the back of the cushion or the lining of the mat underneath the top with ruffle, right sides together, and stitch around making sure that the ruffle is lying flat towards the centre of the article. For a mat, leave an opening on one side to turn the mat through. For a cushion cover, leave the zipper partly open and stitch all the way around. The cushion top is turned through the zipper opening.
6 Turn article to the right side, rounding out the corners. For the mat slip stitch the opening closed. Press.

### Piping

Use this section if trimming with piping.

1 Prepare piping by covering the cord with fabric. If you are using cotton piping cord, wash it first in hot water as it will shrink appreciably.
2 For a 6-mm (¹/4-in) cord and a 12-mm (¹/2-in) seam allowance, you will need a casing 4.5-cm (1³/4-in) wide by the length of your piping. Fabric cut on the cross will go around corners more smoothly. It takes less fabric on the straight grain but the corners will pucker a little.
3 Lay the cord along the centre of the wrong side of the casing. Using the zipper foot on your machine, stitch through the casing close to the cord, but not crowding it because the stitching

*Design for GUM BLOSSOMS CUSHION*
80% actual size

lines to attach it to the cushion will be between this stitching and the cord.

4 Follow steps 3–6 of Ruffles above, but use the zipper foot when stitching the cord. Join the ends neatly or, if the cord is not too thick, stitch across the ends, which have been overlapped and tucked to the inside of the cushion cover.

### A *plain cushion*

1 Place the back and front with the right sides together and, leaving the zipper partly open, stitch around the cushion.
2 Neaten the seam.
3 Turn to the right side through the zipper opening, rounding out the corners neatly.

Complete design

# Brolga wall hanging or cushion

This design is suitable for a wall hanging or a cushion cover. The birds in the wall hanging are twice as big as the given design so you would have to enlarge them (see Designs on page 5). One large bird on its own would also be suitable for a cushion cover. This is one appliqué where you could look for a feather design fabric for the birds. If you do this, then it is a good idea to cut out the appliqué pieces in such a way that you will have the feathers facing the same direction on all pieces of all the birds. The arrows on the templates are a guide for this.

The method given is for the cushion cover. To make the wall hanging, follow the Frogs wall hanging instructions on page 35, first embroidering the sun to go behind the brolgas. You may like to have two 6-mm (¼-in) borders, then a 2.5-cm (1-in) border as pictured facing page 17, instead of one 3.5-cm (1½-in) plain border.

### Embroidered sun

The machine embroidered sun in the centre of the wall hanging is in gold metallic thread. Work it as follows.

1 Find the centre of the wall hanging and mark the guidelines for your embroidery using a quilter's or dressmaker's pencil. The round part of the sun is 9 cm (3½ in) across with the longest rays reaching out another 8 cm (3 in) all around giving you a finished sun of approximately 24 cm (9 in) in diameter. The brolgas' heads and beaks will cover part of this.
2 Using the free-machining technique and gold thread, begin in the centre and stitch in a tight spiral outwards until your sun measures approximately 9 cm (3½ in) across.
3 Stitch the sun's rays by making spikes of varying lengths ranging up to 8 cm (3 in) around the body of the sun.

### Materials

These materials are for a cushion cover 46 cm (18 in) across.

- 75 cm (27 in) of fabric for the background
- 25 cm (9 in) of fabric for appliqués
- small piece of contrasting fabric for wing bands and heads
- Vliesofix®
- Tearaway®

- approximately 60-cm (24-in) square of Pellon or light-weight batting
- beads for embellishing
- ribbons for ties (optional)
- 40-cm (16-in) zipper
- size 20 (50 cm or 20 in) cushion insert
- lace or extra fabric for gathered frill (optional)

## Method

1 Following the instructions for Vliesofix® on page 6, trace the brolga design and apply it to the appliqué fabric. Cut out the pieces.
2 Arrange the appliqués on the background (the brolga's feet on the wall hanging can overlap the border).
3 Iron on Tearaway® backing.
4 Satin stitch the edges of the appliqués.
5 Stitch the beads in place on the wings and eyes. For larger birds, a sequin with a bead to hold it in place makes a good eye.
6 Remove the Tearaway® backing.
7 Quilt the top, if desired (see Quilting by machine on page 12) and make up cushion (see Making up a cushion on page 41).

**Note:** The brolga's legs may be cut from fabric and appliquéd or outlined with satin stitch, and filled in with hand embroidered chain stitch in gold thread as in the photograph. If you choose to embroider, cut a template of the legs from paper and trace the outline on your fabric with a sharp, black, lead pencil. You will not see these lines once the legs are completed, as you will have stitched over them.

Embroidered sun

9 cm (3½ in)

23 cm (9 in)

Actual size pattern

Use the brolga this size for the cushion, double the size for the wall hanging

44

# Autumn Flowers vest

This vest has three appliquéd panels and is lined. You could use strip piecing for the main body of the vest, as in the photograph facing page 32, or make it all in one fabric.

## Materials

These materials are needed for a medium-sized vest.

- commercial pattern for a straight vest in your size
- approximately 1.5 m (1¹/₂ yd) fabric (be guided by the pattern)
- approximately 1.5 m (1¹/₂ yd) lining fabric (be guided by the pattern)
- small pieces of fabric for appliqués
- approximately 2.3 m (2²/₃ yd) of bias binding, either bought or made from the vest fabric.
- seed beads
- six buttons OR use button covering kit (optional)
- Vliesofix®
- Tearaway®

---

### Strip piecing guidelines

- If you want a strip-pieced vest, as shown in the photograph, you will need five co-ordinating fabrics, plus one for the appliqué background. With the exception of the applique strips, all strips should be 5 cm or 2 in (4 cm or 1¹/₂ in finished size) in width (see diagrams)
- The two front appliquéd strips should be 9 cm or 3¹/₂ in (7.5 cm or 3 in finished size) in width. The back appliquéd strip is 11.5 cm or 4¹/₂ in (10 cm or 4 in finished size) in width.
- Two extra 5 cm (2 in) strips from the same material as the appliqué strips, are used in the back. These strips will be against the side seams.
- All of the strips should be the length of the completed vest with allowance for seams at either end.
- For a larger or smaller size vest, you will have to alter the width of the strips in order to match the number of strips in the diagram.

---

## Method

1 Begin by making the three appliquéd strips. Following the instructions for Vliesofix® on page 6, trace and apply the flowers to the appliqué fabric. Cut out the pieces.

Actual size pattern

Make two 19-cm (7¹/₂-in) motifs for each front

*Design for AUTUMN FLOWERS VEST*

45

80% actual size

Make three 16.5-cm (6½-in) motifs for the back

2 Begin at centre front and baste one strip B to the centre front of the lining fabric, wrong sides together, matching the edges exactly. You are constructing the vest on the lining base. It is essential to keep your work absolutely flat and to stitch and press accurately so that you do not pull the vest out of shape.

3 Next is the appliquéd panel. Making sure the appliqué will be below finished neckline, place

Layout for fronts and back        4-cm (1½-in) strips

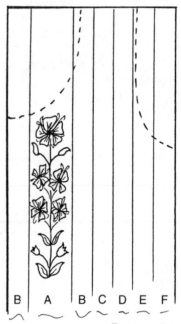

Front appliqué panels are 9 cm (3½ in) wide

**Note:** The two fronts have appliqué only as far as the lowest part of the neck shaping; despite this the strip must be cut to measure from the bottom of the vest to the shoulder. This is the piece that will take most of the neck shaping later.

2 Arrange the pieces on the panels as in the photograph, spacing them out to fit the length.
3 Iron on Tearaway® backing.
4 Satin stitch around the appliqués then work the embroidery and beading.
5 Remove Tearaway® backing.

### Strip-pieced vest

1 Cut out the lining, leaving a generous seam allowance on all sides except the centre front so that the vest can be cut to the correct size when the piecing is completed.

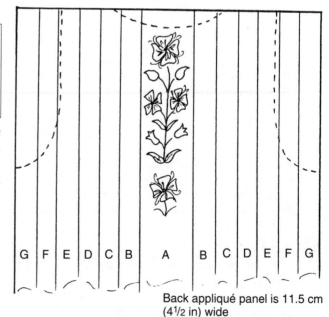

Back appliqué panel is 11.5 cm (4½ in) wide

the right sides of the appliqué panel to right side of first strip and stitch them together onto the lining.

4 Turn the panel over so that the right side is up and press away from the seam line.

5 Put the next strip B on the appliquéd panel edge, right side to right side, and stitch. Turn and press as before.

6 Continue in this way using strips C, D, E and F in order.

7 Complete the other front to match.

8 For the back, begin by placing the central appliquéd panel first and work out from either side of it.

9 When all pieces are together, top stitch 4 mm (1/8 in) from all seams.

10 Now cut all the pattern pieces accurately, leaving a 12-mm (1/2-in) seam allowance on the shoulders and sides.

11 To make up, stitch the shoulder and side seams. Trim the two front fabric seam allowances and one lining seam allowance back to 6 mm (1/4 in). Fold the untrimmed lining seam allowance over the three raw edges and slip stitch into place, thus neatening the inside.

12 If using buttons, make button loops (see glasses case instructions on page 19) and baste into place on the right front.

13 Using bias binding, bind all the raw edges.

14 Stitch on the buttons.

*One colour vest*

1 Cut out the lining fabric using the pattern.

2 Make up the fronts with one 5-cm (2-in) strip in the centre front and the appliquéd panel next.

3 Cut the remaining piece of the front using the pattern and attach to the appliquéd panel.

4 Make up the back with the centre appliquéd piece in place.

5 Baste the fronts and back to linings and treat as one.

6 If desired, you could quilt the two layers together either side of the appliquéd panels and then at 4-cm (1 1/2-in) intervals.

7 Follow the making up instructions, steps 11–14 above.

# Autumn Flowers belt

You can make a belt to match the vest using the same flower design and elongating it by adding more flowers.

The belt is shown in colour facing page 32.

## Materials

- 9 cm (3 1/2 in) x your waist measurement plus 10 cm (4 in) of fabric for background
- backing fabric the same size as the background fabric

Half belt design

47

- 2 strips of medium- to heavy-weight iron-on Vilene, the same size as the background fabric
- 2 strips of bias binding each 9 cm (3½ in) long
- scraps of fabric for appliqués
- Vliesofix®
- seed beads
- 1 x 8-cm (3-in) clasp
- 10 cm (4 in) of Velcro

## Method

1 Following the instructions for Vliesofix® on page 6, trace and apply the design to the appliqué fabric.
2 Arrange the appliqués on the background fabric using the diagram as your guide. Leave 8 cm (3 in) clear of appliqué on both ends and make sure the design does not go over the seam allowance along the length of the belt.
3 Use one piece of the iron-on Vilene to stabilise the appliqué.
4 Satin stitch the appliqués in place.
5 Complete all the embroidery and beading on the appliqués.
6 Fuse the second strip of iron-on Vilene to the backing.
7 Cut four 2.5-cm (1-in) pieces of Velcro and stitch two fluffy pieces on each end of the backing, 9 cm (3½ in) from the end and 1.5 cm (½ in) in from either side.
8 With right side of the backing to right side of the belt, stitch down both sides then turn the right side out.
9 Press carefully and top stitch close to the edges.
10 Bind the raw ends with the bias binding pieces.
11 Stitch the grip side of the four pieces of Velcro in line with the fluffy side and up against the bias binding.
12 Thread a half of the clasp onto each belt end and secure with the Velcro. The Velcro strips will allow for some adjustment.

Join the two dotted lines together to get the pattern for half of the belt

Actual size pattern

*This Tree of Life Quilt is an extended version of the wall hanging.
This is a very special quilt and the flower centres are decorated with tiny
gold domes; it won the Viewers' Choice Award at the Diamond Creek Quilt
and Needlework Exhibition in 1993.*

*The Magpie Quilt has also been adapted from a prize-winning wall hanging. It has no beading, so it is not only beautiful, but also very practical to use on a bed. Make the centre panel on its own as a wall hanging to bring a touch of the bush indoors.*

## Design for AUTUMN FLOWERS BELT

Actual size pattern

# *Jackets: Pheasants and Flowers and Summer Garland*

These two jackets are made from the same pattern, which was adapted from a blouse pattern. Ribbing was added to the cuffs, bottom, neck and front fastening. They are lined, the lining being cut the same as the jacket then attached to it with the ribbing. This makes a very versatile jacket that can be either casual or formal. Any simple jacket or blouse pattern could be used, the fewer seams there are, the easier it is to place the appliqués.

The jackets are shown in colour facing page 33.

## Materials
- jacket or blouse pattern that can be adapted, having as few seams as possible
- fabric for jacket and lining as specified in the pattern
- pieces of fabric for appliqué birds, flowers, branches and butterflies
- ribbing for edges (optional)
- Vliesofix®
- Tearaway®

## Method
1 Cut out the jacket pieces but do not join any seams.
2 Following the instructions for Vliesofix® on page 6, trace and apply the design to the appliqué fabric.
3 Arrange the pieces on the jacket and satin stitch them in place. With the jackets, it is sometimes easier to put the Tearaway® stabiliser on in sections as you work. For example, on the back of the Pheasants and Flowers jacket, first work the birds, then each sleeve. If the Tearaway® lifts off, it is easily ironed on again.
4 Complete all the appliqué, machine or hand embroidery and beading before making up the jacket.
5 Remove Tearaway® backing.
6 Cut out the lining and complete the seams.
7 If you are using ribbing, baste the lining to the jacket, wrong sides together, at the cuffs, neck, fronts and bottom edge before applying the ribbing, otherwise finish the jacket and lining according to your pattern.

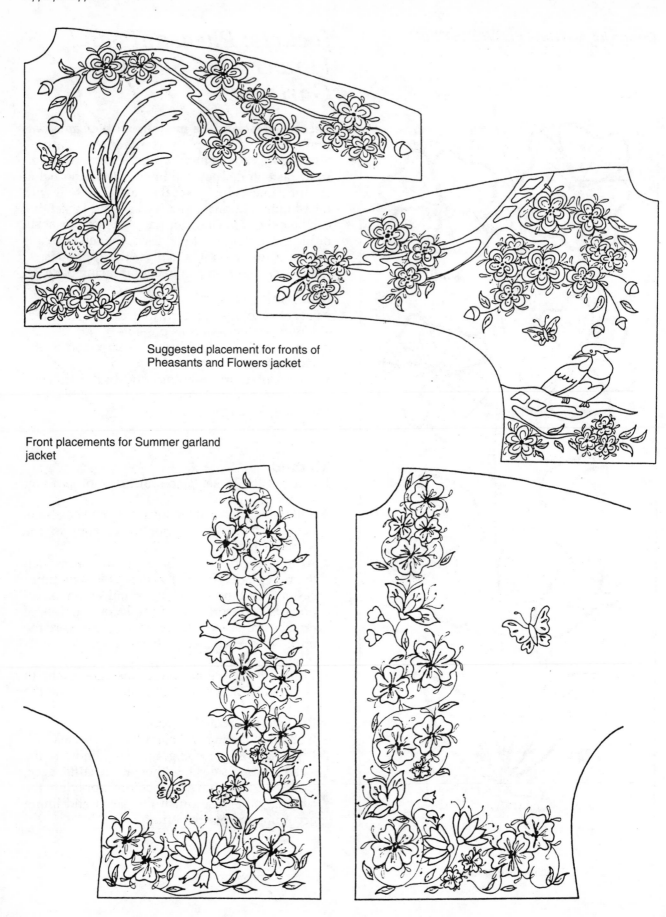

Suggested placement for fronts of
Pheasants and Flowers jacket

Front placements for Summer garland
jacket

*Design for PHEASANTS and FLOWERS JACKET*
80% actual size

Left front

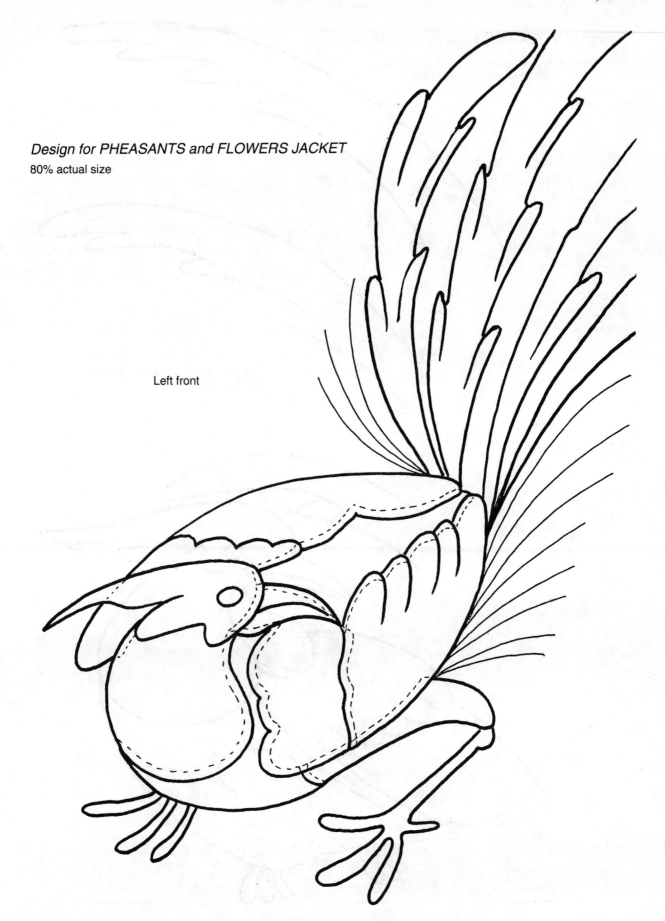

## Design for PHEASANTS and FLOWERS JACKET
80% actual size

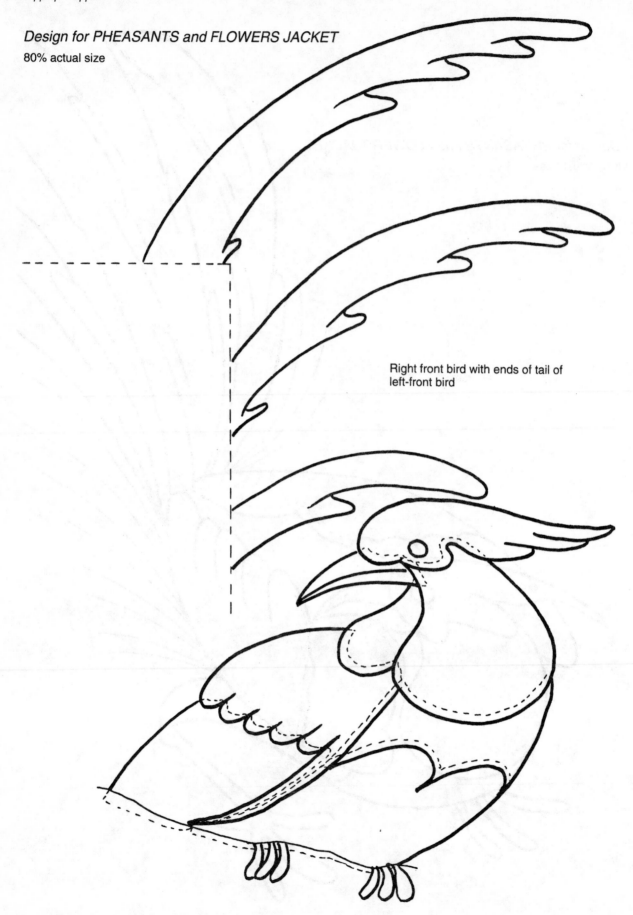

Right front bird with ends of tail of left-front bird

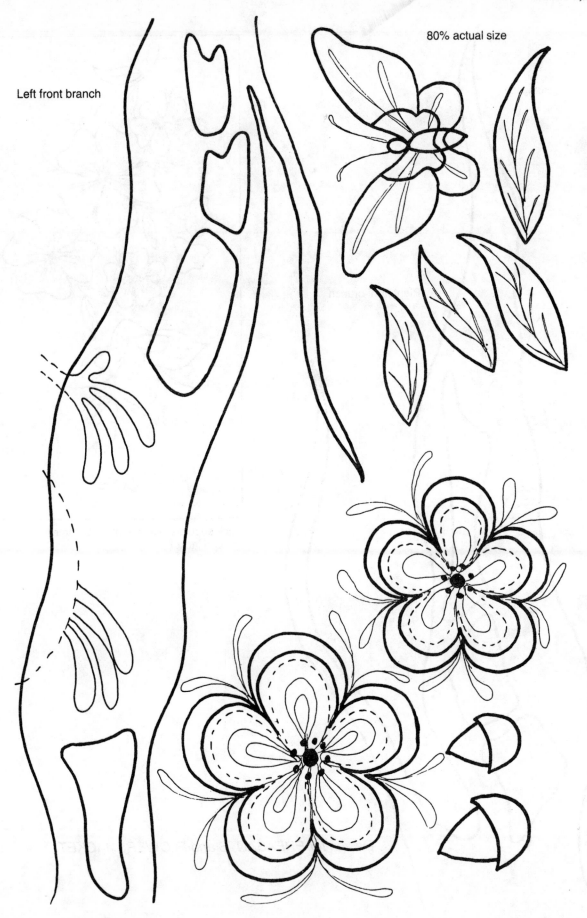

Left front branch

80% actual size

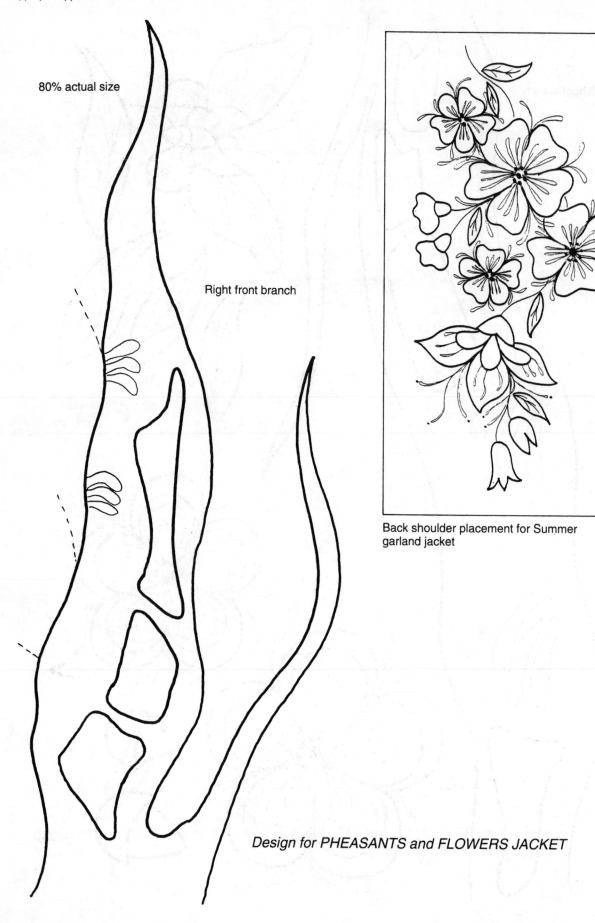

80% actual size

Right front branch

Back shoulder placement for Summer garland jacket

*Design for PHEASANTS and FLOWERS JACKET*

*Design for SUMMER GARLAND JACKET*

Actual size pattern

# Quilts

These quilts require some knowledge of quilt construction, although the appliqué motifs could be used on other projects. The Tree of Life wall hanging, for example, is the centre of the Tree of Life quilt. This pattern is easy to make bigger or smaller just by adding or subtracting more leaves, flowers, etc.

## Method

Using the measurements from the chart, complete all appliquéd sections before making up the quilt. Leave a generous allowance in particular on side strip ends to give yourself a good margin for error. Although the measurements given in the diagrams are those in the actual quilts, keep checking the overall size of your quilt as you progress, measuring each way through the centre of the piece. Use these measurements for the next border length. Do not use the outside edge measurement of your quilt as this measurement can differ from a measurement through the centre line. Working from the edge measurements will result in the quilt not lying as flat as it should.

> **Note:** 'Measure twice cut once' is a good rule to remember.

See Quilting by machine on page 12 for how to put the quilt together and quilting it. The central panels could be quilted in straight-sided diamond shapes (see Marking on page 13) instead of the Cornelli free-machining, if you desire.

# Tree of Life quilt

## Materials

Two fabric measurements are given for fabrics C, D and E. The first measurement is for those who do not wish to have seam lines across the borders. The second measurement, which uses less fabric, will have seams across the borders.

- 2.3 m (2³⁄₄ yd) of plain fabric A
- 2.5 m (2²⁄₃ yd) of dark brown patterned fabric B
- 2.5 m (2²⁄₃ yd), if you want no joins; 1.25 m (1¹⁄₄ yd) with joins, light brown on brown patterned fabric C
- 2.1 m (2¹⁄₃ yd), if you want no joins; 1.05 m (1 yd) with joins, dark floral fabric D

Actual size pattern

*Design for TREE OF LIFE WALL HANGING and QUILT*

- 2.1 m (2¹/₃ yd), if you want no joins; 1.05 m (1 yd) with joins, grey/green fabric E
- small pieces of fabric in toning colours; browns, greens and creams, for appliqués
- gold domes for flower centres (optional)
- 2 m x 2.4 m (80 in x 96 in) batting
- 4.9 m (5¹/₃ yd) of 115-cm (45-in) backing fabric, this will need to be pieced

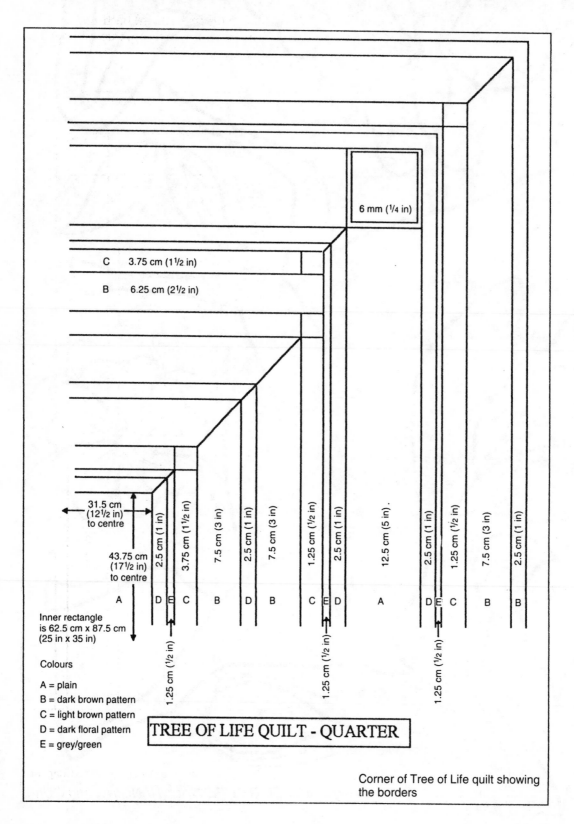

6 mm (¹/₄ in)

C    3.75 cm (1¹/₂ in)

B    6.25 cm (2¹/₂ in)

31.5 cm (12¹/₂ in) to centre

43.75 cm (17¹/₂ in) to centre

Inner rectangle is 62.5 cm x 87.5 cm (25 in x 35 in)

Colours

A = plain
B = dark brown pattern
C = light brown pattern
D = dark floral pattern
E = grey/green

2.5 cm (1 in) — D
3.75 cm (1¹/₂ in) — C
7.5 cm (3 in) — B
2.5 cm (1 in) — D
7.5 cm (3 in) — B
1.25 cm (¹/₂ in) — C
2.5 cm (1 in) — D
12.5 cm (5 in) — A
2.5 cm (1 in) — D
1.25 cm (¹/₂ in) — C
7.5 cm (3 in) — B
2.5 cm (1 in) — B

A    D E C    B    D    B    C E D    A    D E C    B    B

1.25 cm (¹/₂ in)    1.25 cm (¹/₂ in)    1.25 cm (¹/₂ in)

**TREE OF LIFE QUILT - QUARTER**

Corner of Tree of Life quilt showing the borders

# *Magpie quilt*

## Materials

- 2.9 m (3¼ yd) plain, light green fabric A
- 2.5 m (2⅔ yd) green/brown patterned fabric B
- 2.5 m (2⅔ yd), if you want no joins; 1.25 m (1¼ yd) with joins, brown patterned fabric C

- 1 m (1 yd) dark green/cream patterned for borders
- pieces of fabric in black and white for magpies, greens and greys for branches, leaves and gum nuts
- 2.25 m x 2.7 m (90 in x 108 in) batting
- 7.3 m (8 yd) fabric for backing; this will need to be joined in three widths

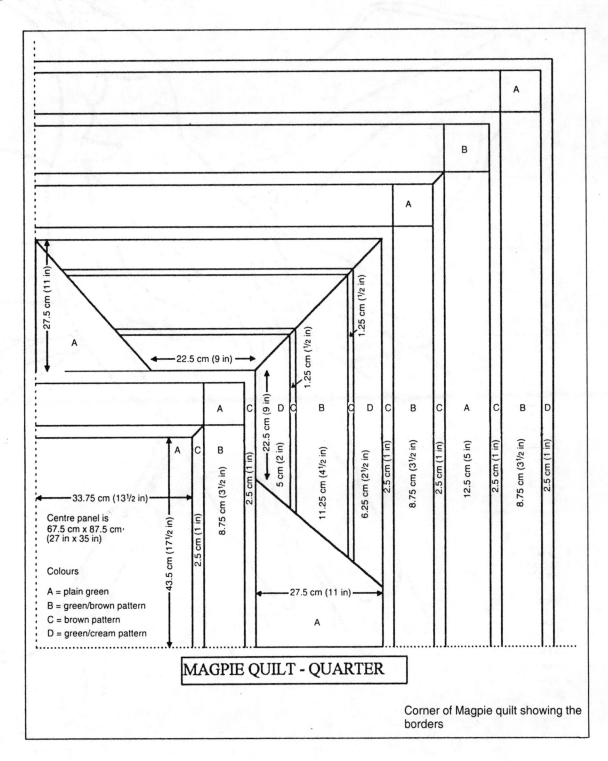

27.5 cm (11 in)

22.5 cm (9 in)

A

1.25 cm (½ in)

1.25 cm (½ in)

22.5 cm (9 in)

5 cm (2 in)

11.25 cm (4½ in)

6.25 cm (2½ in)

2.5 cm (1 in)

8.75 cm (3½ in)

2.5 cm (1 in)

12.5 cm (5 in)

2.5 cm (1 in)

8.75 cm (3½ in)

2.5 cm (1 in)

A  C  D  C  B  C  D  C  B  C  A  C  B  D

A  C  B

A  C  B

2.5 cm (1 in)

8.75 cm (3½ in)

2.5 cm (1 in)

33.75 cm (13½ in)

43.5 cm (17½ in)

27.5 cm (11 in)

Centre panel is
67.5 cm x 87.5 cm·
(27 in x 35 in)

Colours

A = plain green
B = green/brown pattern
C = brown pattern
D = green/cream pattern

**MAGPIE QUILT - QUARTER**

Corner of Magpie quilt showing the borders

*Design for MAGPIE QUILT*

Actual size pattern

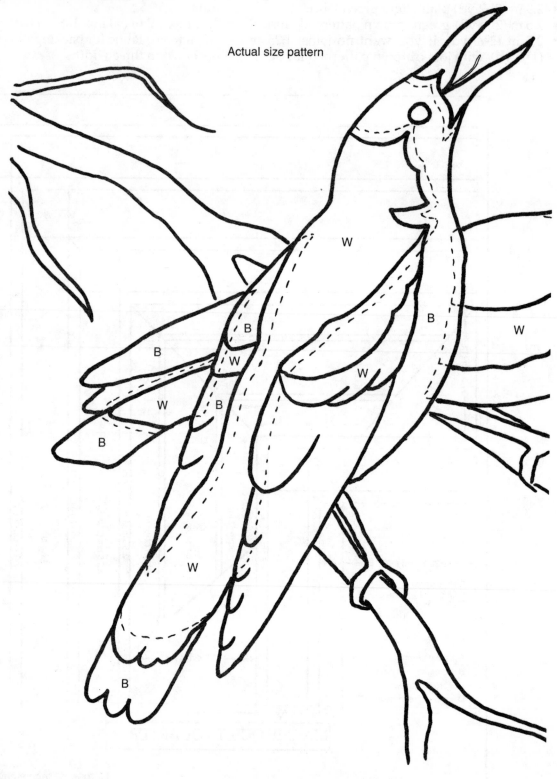

B = black

W = white

# Suppliers

## General

### VICTORIA
Patchwork Affair
205 Upper Heidelberg Road
Ivanhoe 3079
Ph (03) 499 7733

Patchwork House
77 Church Street
Hawthorn 3122
Ph (03) 819 3441

Patchwork Plus
646 High Street
East Kew 3102
Ph (03) 859 9356

Primarily Patchwork
4 Theatre Place
Canterbury 3126
Ph (03) 830 4537

Twinecraft
346 Belmore Road
Balwyn North 3104
Ph (03) 857 6437

### NEW SOUTH WALES
Anne's Glory Box
60 Beaumont Street
Hamilton 2303
Ph (049) 61 6061

Berrima Patchwork & Craft
Hume Highway
Berrima 2577
Ph (048) 77 1382

Lynne's Little Patchwork Shop
156 Baylis Street
Wagga Wagga 2650
Ph (069) 22 3533

The Quilting Bee
Shop 14
Gordon Village Arcade
Pacific Highway
Gordon 2072
Ph (02) 499 2203

### QUEENSLAND
Marguerita's Patch
2/117 Toolooa Street
Gladstone 4680
Ph (079) 72 7620

Patchwork Supplies
43 Gloucester Street
Highgate Hill, Brisbane 4101
Ph (07) 844 9391

The Patchwork Tree
43 Denman Street
Alderley 4051
Ph (07) 356 3866

### SOUTH AUSTRALIA
Hope Valley Haberdashery &
Craft
1220 Grand Junction Road
Hope Valley 5059
Ph (08) 396 2422

The Quilt Basket
102 Main Street
Yankalilla 5204
Ph (085) 58 2720

The Quilters Cupboard
32 Main Street
Hahndorf 5245
Ph (08) 388 7699

### AUSTRALIAN CAPITAL TERRITORY
Calico Patch
Ginninderra Country Crafts
O'Hanlon Place
Ginninderra 2617
Ph (06) 230 2326

Truly Lois
Cnr Victoria & Gladstone Streets
Hall 2618
Ph (06) 230 2415

### WESTERN AUSTRALIA
The Calico House
2 Napoleon Street
Cottesloe 6011
Ph (09) 383 3794

Patchworkers of WA
394 Fitzgerald Street
North Perth 6006
Ph (09) 328 9109

### TASMANIA
The American Patchworks
91 Patrick Street
Hobart 7000
Ph (002) 34 2279

The Quilt Patch
116 St. John Street
Launceston 7250
Ph (003) 31 6531

### NORTHERN TERRITORY
Alice Traders
Schwartz Crescent
Alice Springs 0871
Ph (089) 52 2450

## Beads, sequins, etc

### VICTORA
The Bead Co. of Victoria
336 Smith Street
Collingwood 3066
Ph (03) 419 0636

Beads Galore Pty Ltd
258 Chapel Street
Prahran 3181
Ph (03) 510 5477

Handworks Supplies Pty Ltd
121 Commercial Road
Prahran 3181
Ph (03) 820 8399

### NEW SOUTH WALES
Bead Co. of Australia
497 Elizabeth Street
Surry Hills 2010
Ph (02) 318 2775

Beads Galore Pty Ltd
25a Playfair Street
The Rocks, Sydney 2000
Ph (02) 247 5946

# Further Reading

Stadia Handcrafts
85 Elizabeth Street
Paddington 2021
Ph (02) 328 7900

**QUEENSLAND**
Bead & Trimming Co.
69 Elizabeth Street
Brisbane 4000
Ph (07) 221 1315

**SOUTH AUSTRALIA**
The Bead Shop
190 Goodwood Road
Millswood 5034
Ph (08) 373 1296

**NORTHERN TERRITORY**
Tanami Garden Centre
Paterson Street
Tennant Creek 0860
Ph (089) 62 2809

Many department stores and
haberdashers also carry a range
of beads.

## Threads
Patchwork shops, sewing
machine shops, department
stores and haberdashers usually
have a good range. For
information about stockists of
special threads contact the
following wholesaler:
Madeira Australia
Penguin Threads Pty Ltd
25–27 Izett Street
Prahran 3181
Ph (03) 529 4400

Bawden, Juliet, *The Art and Craft of Appliqué*, Mitchell Beazley, London, 1991.
Brown, Pauline, *Appliqué*, Merehurst Press, London, 1989.
Harker, Gail, *Machine Embroidery*, Merehurst Press, London, 1990.
Hargrave, Harriet, *Mastering Machine Appliqué*, C & T Publishing, California, 1991.
Hargrave, Harriet, *Heirloom Machine Quilting*, C & T Publishing, California, 1990.
Osler, Dorothy, *Quilting*, Merehurst Press, London, 1991.
Todman, Tonia, *Stencilling Book*, Sally Milner, NSW Australia, 1992.

# Index